The Art of Disruption

A Manifesto for Real Change

Magid Magid

First published in the UK by Blink Publishing
An imprint of Bonnier Books UK
80-81 Wimpole Street, London, W1G 9RE
Owned by Bonnier Books
Sveavägen 56, Stockholm, Sweden

www.bonnierbooks.co.uk

facebook.com/blinkpublishing
twitter.com/blinkpublishing

Hardback – 9781788702904
Ebook – 9781788702911
Audio – 9781788703291

A CIP catalogue of this book is available from the British Library.

Printed and bound by Clays Ltd, Elcograf S.p.A.

1 3 5 7 9 10 8 6 4 2

535 is an imprint of Bonnier Books UK
www.bonnierbooks.co.uk

اَلسَّلَامُ عَلَيْكُم

As-salāmu 'alaykum, 'peace be upon you'

This book is dedicated to hooyo macaan (my dearest mother),
my beloved home city Sheffield and
to all those who dare to hope.

CONTENTS

PROLOGUE

From the outside, mine is an unlikely story. I'm a Somali-born, working-class black Muslim immigrant, who fled conflict as a small child and ended up in Sheffield. I grew up being told that people like me weren't made for political office and that I couldn't make a real difference.

Like many people, I grew up in a socially deprived, neglected community that was rife with criminal activity and a lack of opportunities. Not having many role models growing up, the only two posters on my bedroom wall were of Buffy the Vampire Slayer and The Rock. My mum has never really grasped the Western cultural trend of displaying pictures of people you've never met, especially when they're a woman brandishing a sharpened wooden stake and a well-built man standing in his underwear with one eyebrow raised.

With a desire to see, feel and experience things beyond my neighbourhood and the city that was now my home, I became fascinated by travel. My wanderlust led me to order boxloads of holiday brochures from the internet. Finally, after finishing my A-levels and slaving away for six months in factories, working 12-hour shifts, I'd cobbled together enough cash to travel to some incredible places.

I thought that I might work out what I wanted to study at university while I was travelling, but it just didn't happen. What I did know, and what my mum had taught me, was that if I went to uni it would provide me with some amazing opportunities. To cut a long story short, I ended up studying aquatic zoology at Hull University. Admittedly, this was a course I had no interest in pursuing as a career, in a city I knew nothing about, other than the fact I had it on good authority from my mate's dad that it was "an absolute shit-hole", but I took my chances and decided to see the good in the situation. To this date, it's one of the best decisions I've ever made.

After a brief stint starting up a business that ended up in failure, I fell into depression. Hope arrived in the unusual form of an advert for a 32-day medical trial, during which time I made some lifelong friends, as well as discovering my resilience and campaigning ability. At around this point, something in me changed: I just got tired of complaining. And then the rhetoric of hate, fear and division frogmarched UKIP to victory in the 2014 European elections, and I realised that I wanted to do something about it. I decided to stand up for what I believed was right and began to play an active role in my community.

I thought that if I could make my little part of the world in Sheffield a bit better and make a small difference to people's lives, I would have played my part. So I joined the Green Party. I knocked on people's doors. I went to every community event going. And I got elected as a local councillor. Two years later, I became the youngest ever Lord Mayor of Sheffield. I've spent much of the last year as a Green MEP representing God's own country, Yorkshire and the Humber. I still pinch myself every time someone on a stage reads out my name.

But things have not always been smooth sailing. There have been countless people and groups who have tried to put barriers in my way and make life difficult for me. And at times I still get imposter syndrome and find myself thinking, 'They're going to catch me out any moment and realise I'm a fraud!'

From banning Donald Trump from Sheffield and creating a UK-wide suicide prevention charter, to walking someone I've never met before down the aisle at their wedding and having to stick something up my bum on Mount Kilimanjaro (you'll find out what and why later), I've had a lot of weird and wonderful experiences that have shaped who I am today.

During my year as lord mayor, the Sheffield music festival Tramlines asked if I wanted to design a poster with a message to the people of Sheffield that would be displayed around the festival. Not having much time to spare, I quickly came up with something. It was the festival's tenth anniversary and I wanted to create a message of hope. I came up with a series of universal principles that people would relate to, remember and subscribe to. And so Sheffield's Ten Commandments was born. The poster ended up being 12 feet tall and a massive hit. It seemed to resonate with people so much that they started creating their own versions of it and sticking them up on their bedroom walls. Little did I know then that these commandments would later become the template for this book.

I want everyday people to reject the status quo that is failing people like them. Our system is broken, and the establishment is out of touch and out of ideas. Politics shouldn't just belong to the moneyed elite who sit comfortably in lavish offices at the top of ivory towers. It must be made accessible for absolutely everyone, and I try to live that belief every day and in everything I do. Poor representation in politics breeds mistrust and disrespect, and diverse representation builds tolerance and understanding. I know first-hand that coming together and finding a sense of belonging are better than isolation and fear.

If you ever find yourself in a similar position, remember that we cannot afford to bury our heads in the sand. We need to speak out, because staying silent is siding with the oppressor. Every single one of us has a social circle, some form of platform and some degree of influence, even if it's just to our friends, or our parents, or our work colleagues. Speaking truth to power, acting according to our capability and opportunity, whatever that may be, is our collective responsibility. So go out and ruffle the right feathers, ask difficult questions and remind the establishment of your own radical and disruptive power for positive change, whether that's in work, life or politics. Change for the better is not only possible but probable when we come together for the sake of our common values. With conviction in our beliefs and committed action, with unity, strength and compassion, we will build a world that truly works for us all. And there is hope ahead. I'm living proof that even in the most difficult of circumstances, there is hope!

I'm sick to the back teeth of being told not to be 'too political', that I should 'tone it down a bit' or that it's best I don't speak on this or that issue. I don't have the privilege to sit in silence. Have you seen me? I am a black, Muslim immigrant. Have you seen the racism and injustice happening all around us and at the heart of this government, from child poverty and the hostile environment policy to the inaction on climate change? Do you think I could just opt out of being 'too political'? Would my silence, in spite of my platform and opportunity, be fair on people like my mother, my neighbours, my colleagues and everyone else that has faced and continues to face suffering, alienation and marginalisation? No!

Anyone can be an activist, and this book will show you how. When inspirational, decent people combine, the seeds of change begin within society to sprout. In a world that's driving us apart, we need to bring people together with a common purpose. We must work to build a new world, rooted in the aspirations of the young and able to deliver lasting change for all. We must address the defining, unresolved problems of our era and demand urgent change to ensure the future of our planet, whether that means calling for action on climate change, taking Trump to task, combating austerity or defending migrants. We must speak out against injustice,

stand up to racism, hate and intolerance and defend the powerless, disenfranchised and voiceless sections of our society. To achieve all this, we need to do things differently, reach out rather than turn away and choose hope over fear. That is what this book is all about.

MAGID X

I
BE KIND

'My wish for you is that you continue. Continue to be who and how you are, to astonish a mean world with your acts of kindness. Continue to allow humor to lighten the burden of your tender heart.'

Maya Angelou

I love buses. They've always been important to me, and once they are all powered sustainably, they're going to help save the world. Interactions on buses have created iconic moments in 20th-century history: the American civil rights movement was sparked into life on a bus in Montgomery, Alabama, in 1955, when a woman called Rosa Parks refused to accept the status quo. And then in 1963, a young black social worker called Paul Stephenson led a boycott of the Bristol Omnibus Company, after they refused to employ ethnic minorities. The sustained pressure, supported by the wider community in Bristol, caused the company to revoke its ban, heralding a major victory in the struggle for racial equality in Britain. Buses are a melting pot of cultures, outlooks and personalities and can reflect the harmony (or disharmony) of society. They are also the site of many wonderful acts of kindness. And kindness, in whatever form it takes, is always inherently political.

Some of my fondest memories have taken place on Sheffield buses. I remember, aged five or six, forcing my mum to catch double-deckers so I could sit upstairs at the front and pretend I was driving. I'd be the kid singing 'The wheels on the bus go round and round', but everyone does that, right? I saw the world from a different viewpoint perspective on the top of that bus. At street level everything seemed grey, but on the top deck I realised how green and beautiful Sheffield was, how many trees there were.

As a 13-year-old kid, one of my favourite things was heading down to the local bus station, picking a random bus number and then spending the day riding it. I'd see so many different types of people and parts of Sheffield that were so alien to me. I remember thinking that Sheffield was just a load of different villages, some of them posher than others. I was in awe of the places with the massive houses, but many of the people from these areas would be coming into town, catching the same bus with me and sitting next to me. We all had completely different lives, backgrounds and priorities, and the one thing we'd share is the city. Riding buses taught me about the place where I lived more than anyone else could have.

Sometimes those journeys would just be about escapism and I'd listen to music the whole time. But sometimes I'd spend time thinking or people-watching. Sometimes I'd be with my friends and it would feel like a youth club at the back of the bus. We felt protected there, like it was our own kingdom.

We'd be loud and fool around. If you weren't listening to loud hip hop on the bus, you just weren't cool. So I'd be mainly playing Nas, Outkast and 50 Cent, with some Dizzee Rascal thrown in. One of my sisters had got me into that stuff but the other one was really into boy bands and more pop-y stuff so I grew up loving that too, only I kept that quiet. There'd be times when I'd be listening to 'Wannabe' by the Spice Girls on my headphones – quietly, you understand – and if one of my mates asked me what I was listening to, I'd be like, 'Er, this Dizzee tune is a banger, bruv!'

In hindsight, we were probably super annoying to everyone else on the bus. Along with the local park, our actual youth club and my friend Nageeb's grandma's house, the back of the bus was one of a few sacred places that we felt was ours. If you think about it, a bus is where it's at when you don't have much money: you're warm, you've got shelter, you're seeing different things and, depending on which bus you're on, you're also getting free entertainment.

In my early twenties, I'd take the bus to work; I didn't mind where I sat and tried to remember what it felt like to be the kid at the front or among the teens at the back: everyone has their own bus vibe, and

I appreciate that. I've witnessed some of the most simple and beautiful acts of kindness on Sheffield's buses. If you take buses, I bet you can think of many examples of your own: like when someone's shopping bag splits open and fruit and veg starts rolling around the bus, and people jump up to help, or when someone helps an elderly person off the bus. With the ice broken, the atmosphere changes, people start chatting and the magic starts to happen. When I was younger, I began to fall in love with passengers' quirks and started trying to think of creative ways to strike up conversations. But I didn't have the courage to do it and would then regret not saying anything. Now, things are different and I do.

Everyone has at least one bus story to tell, whether good or bad – or both, for that matter. I've got a few, but here's one I want to share with you that demonstrates the value of kindness and how it can change things, big and small.

One spring morning in 2018, I was rushing to the bus stop to catch the number 20 (which, to my disappointment, wasn't a double-decker), on my way to work. I smiled at the driver, tapped my pass on the electronic reader and offered a cheerful 'Hi!' (yes, we still do this up North). I scoped out the other commuters, gave a friendly nod to the regulars I'd become acquainted with and chose the most interesting looking person to sit with. On this day, there was a woman wearing the exact same green Dr Martens boots as me. Well, maybe a couple of sizes smaller. She was the last person I'd expect to be wearing them, too: an old lady, perhaps in her mid-eighties, frail but wearing killer red lipstick. I remember thinking that she stood out as much as a Labour Party supporter in Surrey.

I headed straight over to the seat next to her with the biggest grin on my face, gesturing to both of our shoes excitedly and saying, 'Nice boots – you've got great taste!' She smiled and we spent the journey talking about boots and the weather, before naturally moving on to discussing whether Theresa May was the worst prime minister the country had ever had.

Her name was Delores, but she insisted I called her 'Dee'. And from then on, I'd see Dee every morning on my commute to work. She'd tell me stories about how she'd been the top saleswoman at Cole Brothers (a well-known Sheffield department store, which was sold a few times before ending up as a branch of John Lewis) and even won awards for her efforts. She also told me with a twinkle how she'd used to love going out dancing with her friends every Friday, even though she wasn't as good as her friend Emily, who she described as having 'snake hips' and would attract all the good-looking men. We'd exchange stories about our favourite places in Sheffield and we'd talk a lot about food, with Dee even going as far as saying that she could cook better than Mary Berry!

As forthcoming as Dee was about almost every subject, I noticed that the one thing she never talked about was her family. Sometimes you get a feeling that when someone doesn't want to talk about a subject that usually comes naturally to other people, there might be a sad story behind it. Feeling conscious of not wanting to upset her, I never brought it up.

Every weekday morning I'd greet her with the same chirpy 'Good morning, Dee!' – I was probably too chirpy at 8:30 in the morning, but it never failed to put a smile on her face. For some months, we continued to exchange stories, laughs and sweet treats. But then a few days went by and I didn't see Dee. A week turned into a month. Eventually I moved house and no longer caught the number 20 bus. I was sad not to see Dee anymore, but often thought about her. I missed my bus buddy.

Five months later, early in my term as Lord Mayor of Sheffield, I received an email:

Hi,

Apologies if I've got the wrong person here, but if you are the Magid that gets the number 20 bus, wears the green Docs and would regularly speak with a lady named Delores, then I've sadly got some bad news to share with you. I'm a nurse and have been caring for Delores for the past five months, until she sadly passed away last week due to cancer.

During my time caring for Delores, she would always tell me stories about you and how you were bus buddies. She kept saying how charming, funny and, at times, loud you were. I just wanted to let you know how much of an impact you had on Delores. She has been living alone for the past five years and has no family. She was really isolated and lonely, and she told me the only reason she used to catch the bus in the morning was for you to say good morning to her, because no one else did. It probably wasn't a big deal to you, as I suspect you speak to a lot of people, but to Delores it meant the world because you cared. Thank you for being so kind.

She always mentioned that she knew the new lord mayor, but sadly, I didn't believe her until I saw you in the paper today. I'm really sorry to be the bearer of bad news, but thank you.

I'm not telling you this story to make you think, 'What a great lad that Magid is! He was nice to a lovely, lonely lady.' Rather, I'm sharing Dee's story because it taught me that it's amazing what a single kind word or act can do. You see, there are a lot of people who are hurting inside but smiling on the outside, including people you know are dealing with some stuff and others who are battling adversity that you know nothing about. Lots of us are carrying burdens, feeling lonely and – sometimes – fighting for our lives. Sure, my exchanges with Dee touched me, but when I learned how much they meant to her they ended up meaning a great deal to me, too. One simple act of kindness can lift someone's spirits, breathe hope and meaning into their life, heal them a little and help get them through the day, and that can make all the difference.

*　*　*

Personally, I'm not sure where I'd be without kindness.

Mine is an unlikely story. I'm a black, Muslim refugee and people like me were not crafted for public office. Never in my or my mum's wildest dreams would we have imagined that I would become the youngest lord mayor in the history of Sheffield, my home town. Nor could I have ever imagined getting elected to represent Yorkshire and the Humber at the European Parliament – especially at a time when so much was at stake, with Britain, Europe and the democratic world teetering on the brink of chaos!

My story was made possible because I've been fortunate enough to receive immeasurable kindness from so many people, some of which will appear in this book. I've been helped by a thousand hands, supported by ten thousand hugs and emboldened by one hundred thousand voices. And this is the simple reason why compassion and kindness is at the heart of everything I do.

Despite all the dangerous rhetoric you hear from the far-right press, no one just chooses to leave their home, their family, their friends and their community if there is any other choice. Believe me when I say that we, my family, like many others, didn't choose to leave everything behind to make anyone else's lives difficult. But what choice did my mother have? In 1994, Somalia was in the grip of a devastating civil war. So, with nothing but her courage, hope and self-less determination, she made the decision to flee our home and travel to Ethiopia.

Somehow she kept me, then five years old, completely oblivious to the war that was being waged on our doorstep – I just remember moving from place to place a lot. My mum doesn't want to talk about these things – I think it brings back too many difficult memories. My auntie is a bit more forthcoming and tells me stories about fleeing from gunshots and jumping over dead people – really unspeakable things. There are some things that upset my auntie even now, like if I walk around wearing any sort of camouflaged clothing.

It wasn't until I was in my early teens that I discovered the full horror of what had taken place in my homeland. How the President Siad Barre, whose rule had become more and more dictatorial in the 1980s, had triggered the civil war by clamping down on clan-based groups that were opposed to him. How a number of rebel groups took over different parts of the country, including the United Somali Congress (USC), who ousted Barre from Mogadishu before violently splintering into warring tribal factions. This was followed by widespread attacks on civilians, who were targeted by the warring sides on the basis of their clan identity. Peaceful protestors who appealed to end the fighting were murdered. And then there was the scale of the humanitarian crisis – the sheer number of people who fled and the thousands who remained that perished in the famine. Up to half a million people died and over a million more, including my family, were displaced.

Soon after we left Somalia, we were separated from my auntie. This was before mobile phones and there were so many people trying to make it across the border – it must have been terrifying for my mum, but we were eventually reunited before we crossed into Ethiopia.

I have happy memories of being there, of playing with lots of other children in a housing area that was a kind of holding area for migrants. We'd wrap a bag onto a stick and run around for hours with it, as if we were playing with real balloons. I've always tried to make the most of what I have and find joy in it – it's something all kids do that adults sometimes forget.

We were in Ethiopia for eight months while we waited to see where on earth we would end up, before we were granted asylum in Sheffield. We didn't have access to a phone but my mum did have a tape recorder, and she used it to make long recordings explaining where we were and how we were doing. We still used the tape recorder when we got to Sheffield and my mum used to really hold those tapes dear – her father has since passed away, but his voice is still on them.

It was my mum's sense of hope and resilience that helped us make it to the UK. But to me at the time, it felt that no sooner had we reached Ethiopia, we were boarding a plane bound for a place called Sheffield. My only memory of our arrival was that it was raining, and it didn't take too long to realise that this weather was the default setting for this part of the world. I also had a feeling that I'd later come to know as euphoria, like all of this was an adventure. Maybe that's why I've always thought Sheffield looks prettier in the rain.

Sheffield has a proud history of taking in resettled refugees. With the support of the city council and dozens of community organisations, it became the first 'City of Sanctuary' as part of a movement dedicated to building a sense of welcome and hospitality for refugees and asylum seekers. For the first couple of months we were put up in a house in Darnall, a suburb in east Sheffield. Then we were resettled in a semi-detached house in Burngreave, (or the chocolate side of Sheffield as I like to call it), an inner-city district in the north-east of the city that was home to a diverse community. It was heavily bombed during the war by Zeppelins and major rebuilding work took place in the late 1940s and early 1950s. Many immigrants from countries like Pakistan and Yemen moved to the area to help construct new houses across the city.

There was a lot of optimism and hope when I first arrived, and I remember being really excited. There is something special and warm about Sheffield – I've always felt it. The fact that it had been willing to stand up and provide a safe haven for people who were fleeing conflict mattered more and more to me over time, as I began to understand where we were from, where we had travelled to and why. Now, I feel so lucky that we came here.

We couldn't speak a word of English when we got to Sheffield, but as a kid this didn't really matter, and it didn't stop me from making friends – I was curious and wanted to explore and play. A kid called Sammy, who was of Yemeni descent but born and bred in Sheffield, introduced me to a game called 'curby' that was really popular among kids in the city. The idea was to chuck a football across the street towards the kerb; if you hit it and it bounced back into the road, you got a point. If you missed, it was the other person's turn. Knowing how to play this game meant there were suddenly loads of kids to play with.

Things were more difficult for my mum, who now had to raise her children in a completely new country. She took weekly English classes at the local college, but it fell to my sister Hanan and I to take on extra responsibilities, like form-filling and translation, that most children our age didn't have to do.

Burngreave had the sort of social issues you'd expect in any disadvantaged place in the country in the mid-1990s and early 2000s: anti-social behaviour, drugs, daylight robberies and stabbings were commonplace. I remember a family nearby that had an Alsatian called Tyson and it scared the living daylights out of me. Come to think of it, there were a lot of frightening dogs in the area, all of which had tough names like Brick, Rambo and Bruiser. They would roam around the neighbourhood like they owned the place – some, like Tyson, were known to bite people – and the owners didn't seem to care. I always made sure I had my trainers on rather than my school shoes, because sometimes the dogs would chase and you'd have to sprint and jump over fences to escape them. I learned pretty quickly that you can't run fast in your school shoes! It could be tough trying to convince my teacher why I was late. I'd say, 'I was just trying to run away from Tyson', but I knew my excuse probably sounded made up. Also, even if she believed that what I was saying was true, I could tell that she didn't understand – she was from a nice area, where people had nice dogs with nice names like Apricot, Poppy or Buddy.

But it was in this environment that I learned a lot about friendship, belonging and the value of kindness and compassion. One of the best things about the community I grew up in was how culturally diverse it was – I never felt out of place or like I didn't belong. At primary school, I made friends with kids whose parents had come to Britain from all sorts of places, like Pakistan, Yemen and Jamaica.

THE ART OF DISRUPTION

One of my favourite teachers at school, which I started soon after we arrived in Sheffield, was a Jamaican lady called Miss Simpson. We were her first-ever class, and whenever it was someone's birthday, she would buy presents and throw a party in the classroom. She thought that every child should have a birthday party and not all of their parents would be able to afford one. She can't have had much money, but she paid for it all and made every child feel special, like they belonged here and that they mattered. A lot of people do things for the sake of it or because it's part of their job, but she genuinely wanted the best for us all. She'd always take that extra step, and she'd come over and chat to my mum and the other kids' parents. It was the first time that someone in Sheffield who wasn't in my immediate family really cared about me.

When I was 15, I saw Miss Simpson at a friend's cousin's funeral and went over to her. It had been years since I'd seen her and I remember thinking that she hadn't seemed to age at all – I wondered if there was something really special about Jamaicans! She was really pleased to see me, even though the circumstances were so sad. I got in touch with some friends who were in her class and we all went out with her for dinner. After that, she'd text me a couple of times each year, to see how I was doing. When I became lord mayor, I invited her to my inauguration and seeing her face smiling up at me meant a lot.

My mum valued education above everything else – for her, it was the route to a future with security and a good income, and it was something she never really had. And I know it's a stereotype but for her, like many immigrant parents, the only acceptable careers were medicine, law or engineering – she wouldn't tolerate anything less. I couldn't see it at the time, but I later realised that she just wanted what was best for me, like any parent would. Being a single mum trying to raise children in a tough environment couldn't have been easy. She was always a bit suspicious of my behaviour, and it's true that I got up to some shit I wasn't proud of – but then again, everything I was doing must have seemed completely alien to her, which made the whole parent-teenager relationship doubly difficult. We were so different culturally that at times it felt like there was a sea between us, but all I was doing was trying to find my way. It could be frustrating – I thought this was the life she wanted for me, but at times it didn't feel like it.

I remember logging onto the internet on a school computer for the first time – it completely changed my life. I listened to a lot of pirate radio and began to download music from the internet. I was blown away by how much I could access, so I started a little side hustle. I'd buy a box of 60 cheap blank CDs from somewhere like Asda and burn hip hop compilations onto them, because that's what everyone was after but they couldn't find that sort of music on the radio. I called them 'Magid'z Master Mix' (I got up to 'Volume 7' by the time I left school) and would flog the CDs for £1.50 a pop. I used to make around £45 a week, and in those days, that was a lot of money – definitely more pocket money than my friends would get – so I'd just spend it all on sweets and share them with my mates. I'm talking Hubba Bubba, Rainbow Drops, Kinder eggs, Fizz Wiz and my all-time favourite, the pick 'n' mix. I remember coming home with a couple of big bags of sweets and my mum being really suspicious. She said, 'Where are you getting the money from to buy all these sweets? You certainly ain't getting it from me.' I was just a kid who was trying to make a few quid and have a bit of fun, but my mum was completely baffled by it all.

While my friends and fellow students went to the same college – Longley Park Sixth Form College – I chose a different path after leaving secondary school. I think it was my sense of adventure that prompted me to apply to Tapton Sixth Form on the other, and more affluent, side of the city – I wanted to go somewhere completely different, where I would learn new things and meet different people. In hindsight, although I had decent GCSEs and got in on my own merits, I can't help but think I was also satisfying some sort of diversity quota.

On my first day at Tapton, I realised that it was going to be very different to my school experience to this point. Not only were the vast majority of students white and British, but they played bizarre sports that I'd never heard of, like lacrosse. I remember staring on, baffled, as teams ran around a pitch waving sticks and thinking, 'Wait till I tell the boys back home about this.' It was wild to see how people lived on the other side of town. While I was at Tapton, I made a real effort to mix with people from different backgrounds; some of them welcomed me with open arms, but others took it upon themselves to let me know I didn't belong there. Although I left Tapton after a year and rejoined my mates at Longley Park, I focused on the positives of my experience there – I had learned that regardless of which part of the city you live in, you can always find lovely, kind-hearted people.

For me, the key to all those early interactions was kindness. No matter what people looked like or how wealthy they were, if they were kind people there was a good chance that we'd become friends. It didn't need to be any more complicated than that. I can see it in young kids now: if they feel good around one another and they like doing things together, they become friends. They don't notice what skin colour people have, what clothes they are wearing or what job their parents have, and sometimes they don't even notice if the other kid does not speak their own language – all they know is that they've made a friend. As we grow up, it is easy to forget just how powerful that initial feeling of connection is. Building bridges with strangers can become harder; we can become isolated from others and fearful of new and different people. And yet I believe that we all yearn for connection, even if we don't show it.

* * *

A good friend of mine ran his campaign to be students' union president at the University of Sheffield on the simple but effective slogan, 'Because I said Hi!' It was a straightforward but powerful idea that reminds me of my friendship with Delores. Reaching out and saying hello to people is the first step in any relationship. Like everyone, I often feel lonely, even though I had my family close by and made friends easily when I was growing up. But knowing that I can break myself out of this loneliness by choosing to interact cheerfully with people and listen to what they have to say is what makes a lot of things in my life bearable. I put myself out there and try to connect with people emotionally. Opening yourself up to hurt is a brave thing to do, but it helps me fully experience my vulnerability and not be owned by the fear that others will reject me for it. I think too many people have learned to live with their heads down, not wanting to burden others with their feelings or to open themselves up to difficult situations. Somehow, not wanting to rely on others has become associated with strength.

But then I remember what the psychologist and TED Talk sensation Brené Brown once said: 'Somehow we've come to equate success with not needing anyone. Many of us are willing to extend a helping hand, but we're very reluctant to reach out for help when we need it ourselves. It's as if we've divided the world into "those who offer help" and "those who need help". The truth is that we are both.' It is true: we are both helpers and helped. And when I remember this, I feel lifted. I remember what it was like to be a child and make a friend, and find the courage to reach out to others.

We all possess a magic power in our capacity to reach out and make friends. Underneath it all, we are just kids who need kindness, with kindness of our own to give to others. We forget this because our world is full of harshness and fear – the society children are introduced to as they grow up focuses on competition, external markers of 'success' and straight-up greed, at the expense of community, solidarity and authenticity. That's exactly why we need *you*. We need your energy, passion and unique voice. We need you to be the person to go up to someone and say 'Hi!' We need your thoughts and feelings, your secret passions and quirks. The world is full of people pretending to be someone they are not, and I think authenticity can see us through.

The key is compassion. Yes, we are living through polarising and difficult times, where we may encounter events, words and people that infuriate us. But we need to be strong, to be understanding, to work collaboratively and, most importantly of all, to show compassion. Whatever you want to achieve or change, let compassion be the biggest driving force. Other things may take you partway through a project, but compassion is a sure-fire way to get you to the end. It's limitless and all-encompassing, especially in the case of charity, politics or protest: if compassion doesn't drive you, then you're either in the wrong line of work or you need to start over. And you don't need to do much to find that compassion, in all honesty – you just need to live in the real world.

During my term as lord mayor, I regularly received letters from schoolchildren. The kindness and natural curiosity in some of those letters really kept me going in the dark times, and there were many of those, but I also felt like my desire to be compassionate had a knock-on effect.

While I definitely didn't succeed in uniting all of Sheffield, I'm pretty confident that I was a breath of fresh air in a room full of old farts. And that, in itself, caused quite a lot of trouble, because some people were not always as compassionate towards me or supportive of my approach during my term in office. But what I discovered was that not only did I receive more love than hate, but that the compassion of others helped to keep me going, along with my compassion for myself. I tell people to always remember to show yourself compassion first and let it be a light to guide others who may be struggling.

Kindness is bold, brave and politically radical: in both small gestures and wider structural policies, it has the power to change someone's life – and to change the world.

II
DON'T BE A PRICK

'Ignorance and prejudice are the handmaidens of propaganda. Our mission, therefore, is to confront ignorance with knowledge, bigotry with tolerance, and isolation with the outstretched hand of generosity. Racism can, will, and must be defeated.'

Kofi Annan

When I was elected lord mayor, I quickly found out that people either love me or hate me, but either way they have a passionate opinion of me. My critics used to say I was always attention-seeking. And, to be frank, they're 100 per cent right – I'm literally peacocking! I try to get as much attention as possible for what I'm talking about, the causes I'm championing and the change I'm trying to bring about, but I try to do it as constructively as possible.

It was Maya Angelou who said, 'People may not remember exactly what you did, or what you said, but they will always remember how you made them feel' and that couldn't be more true, especially in the times we live, where life moves so fast and we all suffer from information overload. I always try to engage people on an emotional level, grab their attention and then offer them important information and a topical message that elevates essential causes, demanding a better world. I carry myself in everything I do. It was never my intention to be seen as some sort of irreverent character – it was about being as authentic as possible and giving my honest opinion. Lord mayors have traditionally been of the 'don't rock the boat' persuasion, but I'm not down with that – I never have been.

I am, however, in favour of what I call a 'Don't Be a Prick' approach to everyday life, which starts with five basic requirements:

1. Don't be discriminatory
2. Don't be dishonest
3. Don't be arrogant
4. Don't be cruel
5. Don't be immoral

My life changed a lot when I became lord mayor, but I always tried to keep these five things in mind. Even my morning routine was shaped by it.

I would wake up each day at 7am and think 'Oh God!' when all the things I had to do that day ran through my mind. But then I'd snap out of it with a bit of music, maybe some Alabama Shakes or some French hip hop that Spotify kept recommending me. And then I'd jump into a cold shower. I hate it. But after stumbling on some YouTube videos about the massive health benefits of taking cold showers, I'm determined to believe that this will somehow change my life for the better. Also, starting my day with something so uncomfortable makes me think, 'If I can get through this, everything else will be fine.'

I still don't have breakfast. I know it's a rookie mistake, but I'm just not hungry – plus, I'd rather stay in bed for an extra 20 minutes. I did have a mint Cornetto one morning this week – it was in the freezer and I didn't have the patience for anything else.

Being lord mayor meant that I had the great fortune to have a chauffeured car at my disposal. One the first day I met Carl, my driver and now my friend, he parked up outside my place. When I walked out of the door, I heard the neighbours' kids excitedly shouting 'Hello, Mr Mayor!' Carl tried to open the rear passenger door for me, but I wasn't having any of it. He still tries to open the door sometimes, but when he does I spot what he's doing and will sneak in the other door, which makes him smile and frown at the same time.

Carl has got used to me stopping outside bus stops and offering lifts to people in Sheffield who look like they need it. I can't have a car all to myself – what would be the point in that? We've taken people to job interviews, doctor's appointments and nightclubs. During my time as mayor, it was really important to me to make sure that I hadn't forgotten where I'd come from, or what life was like for my neighbours, friends and constituents. Inviting people into my car was a really important part of that.

However, on the days when I had a little more time, I liked to take the bus. I would sit at the back, just as I did as a teenager, and it became a make-shift office space. It was lovely when people said hello, but some journeys could turn into a bit of a surgery, with me taking notes as people came up and told me their issues. Some people would have questions, while others just wanted to tell me what they thought about me or chat about something happening in Sheffield. They were all friendly – well, as friendly as you can be on a weekday morning.

But I know that it can sometimes turn out differently. During my time as lord mayor, I tried to implement policies that promoted kindness and to help people see the importance of not being a prick, but that didn't stop racists from sending me letters and tweets.

If you are considering becoming a racist, try to think about using your time more constructively – baking or mountain climbing, perhaps. Nothing good ever comes from being a racist. Martin Luther King famously said, 'I look to a day when people will not be judged by the colour of their skin, but by the content of their character,' and that's how it should be. I believe racism is 100 per cent learned behaviour, and so believe it can also be unlearned.

The recent #BlackLivesMatter protests across the world have exposed the dismal record of race-based violence, discrimination and harassment, not only in the US but here in the UK too. Racism is everywhere in the UK, from the workplace, the press, our education establishments and right through to those who should be protecting us, particularly the police and the government. An abundance of black British people, who mostly have experienced racism at a micro, macro, and systematic level, exist and battle it every day to different degrees.

Black communities in the UK are subjected to areas which have poorer access to schools, housing, healthcare, clean air quality, cultural venues, libraries and public services. Black young people in the UK are less likely to have access to opportunities and secure employment and black families are more likely to be affected by government cuts and austerity.

The #BlackLivesMatter movement was founded to establish meaningful change and to end systemic racism. Here are three ways that will help tackle racism:

1. Educate yourself. If you're not black, one of the most important things you can do right now is to learn something about the situation. Read up on why people have been protesting and how you can be part of the change. Racism is real and being non-racist is not enough. We all have to be anti-racists, which means actively fighting against racism rather than being passively sympathetic.

2. Make the realities of British imperialism/colonialism and systemic racism a compulsory part of the school curriculum.

3. The government needs to get serious about tackling racial injustices and creating an equal society. Racism is a systemic issue and needs a systematic approach to defeat it and justice needs to be at the heart of it.

And now, more than ever, we should be focusing on the things that unite us, not that divide us. We've got so much more in common than you think.

* * *

DON'T BE A PRICK

There's been a massive rise in hate crime (meaning crime that's committed on the basis of someone's race, gender identity, sexual orientation, religion, disability or any other perceived difference) since the 2016 EU referendum. And I'm not just talking about statistics here – I've seen the change. The government reacted by launching the 'Hate Crime Action Plan', which was built around five themes: preventing hate crime by challenging beliefs and attitudes; responding to hate crime within our communities; increasing the reporting of hate crime; improving the support for victims of hate crime; and increasing our understanding of hate crime. When I was a city councillor, I played a lead role in working with different social organisations to put a strategy together to fight it.

I remember one of the things the action plan highlighted was where hate crimes take place the most: online, on public transport and in the places people go out in the evenings. I've lost count of how many racist incidents I've witnessed on a night bus and usually, bus drivers either didn't know what to do, pretended not to notice or just didn't give a shit. When I was working on the hate crime strategy, I made it a priority to engage with the local bus companies and to ensure that they trained their bus drivers in how to spot a hate crime, what to do in that situation and how to report it.

For some reason, some people don't like it when people speak a language other than English on a bus. All the incidents I witnessed (and still witness, for that matter) followed a similar pattern: someone talks in a foreign language on their phone, and then someone else reacts with something along the lines of 'We're in England, why aren't you speaking English?', in a volume that can vary from a barely audible mutter to a shout. It's either that or 'Go back to where you came from.' Some people also don't like it when other people wear items of clothing that they're not famil-iar with, in which case you tend to hear things like 'What's that dirty rag doing on your head?'

Witnesses don't know how to react in these kinds of situations, so they panic and freeze. And it's not necessarily their fault for not reacting – it's a difficult circumstance to find yourself in. Each situation is different, but talking to the victim, encouraging oth-ers to do so and not engaging with the perpetrator is one option that can work. If it is possible and safe to do so, slowly presenting a physical barrier between the perpetrator and the victim, without inviting conflict, can prevent the situation from escalating.

If the situation has become violent and you've had suitable training, restrain them. I had to do this on a bus once, using my Brazilian jiu-jitsu experience to restrain someone while we waited for the police, as they attempted to physically attack someone else. My main priority was to make sure the victim felt protected and knew that the abuse would stop.

In that case, I reported the incident to the police who arrived on the scene, but I'd usually report a hate crime to the bus driver. However, reporting them in this way has had mixed results – when I'd follow it up with the bus company, they'd sometimes have no record of the incident. In those cases, I'd then report the incident to the police, but once they knew about it, I'd encounter more issues. Some of them wouldn't know what a hate crime was, and sometimes I'd be told that they didn't have any way of logging them. So I would take it further still, to the city council. You have to stamp out racism and you can't give it oxygen. Allowing it to go unchecked legitimises it and encourages people to think it's ok.

I realise racism has always been there, but it felt like some people didn't feel brave enough to spout racist abuse until they felt their opinions had been validated by the outcome of the EU referendum in 2016 and then the subsequent rise of Boris Johnson, who is happy to say some of the most racist, xenophobic, sexist and homophobic things. Meanwhile, we've got an American president who is doing the same thing on the other side of the Atlantic, and to the east we see the rise of right-wing populism across Europe. This political climate normalises racism; it almost feels like politicians get rewarded with power and high office because they say racist things. And then people react by thinking, 'Well, it must be alright to feel and act the way that I am.' While I was lord mayor, a parent of a black kid told me that their child had been told by another child, 'We voted to leave, so you need to go back to where you came from.' I know they would have learned it from their parents, but this kind of thing cannot go unchallenged. Incidents like this must be reported to the school, who should notify the headteacher, the governors and the local education authority.

I understand that people are hurting – they're struggling for lots of reasons and they want change, but I think their anger and frustration is misdirected. The Tory government has to bear some of the responsibility – austerity has devastated so many communities and left a lot of people behind. Massively privileged members of the cabinet are implementing draconian policies from their ivory towers, completely removed from the vulnerable people that will be hit hardest. They just don't understand the plight of people in disadvantaged communities.

To make things worse, they then connect with white working-class supporters by scapegoating migrants and refugees for being the cause of their situation. This cynical fear-mongering makes people suspicious of those who don't look like them; in reality, immigrants and white working-class people who have had their communities devastated by austerity have more in common with each other than those at the top who are making the decisions. It's the age-old strategy of divide and conquer, and it's all fuelled by fear. That's why I try and focus on hope – it's the antidote to fear.

Hearteningly, one incident of racist abuse I witnessed was met head-on by three teenagers who stood up to it and said, 'You're bang out of order.' As a result, adults nearby were encouraged to get behind them. Sometimes you need a leader to take charge of a situation and empower others to act. I get that it's usually easier not to get involved and sidestep the risk of getting smacked. I also get that some people will be having a shit day and don't want to make it worse. But just think about the possibility that the next victim could be your colleague, your best mate, your teacher or a member of your family. As Martin Luther King wrote in his 'Letter from Birmingham Jail', having been jailed for staging a sit-in against racism, 'Injustice anywhere is a threat to justice everywhere.'

Like a lot of black people in the public eye, especially those who dare to challenge the status quo, I get a lot of online abuse as well as the occasional death threat. I'm not going to lie – it's pretty shit to face so much hate, although I try hard to brush it off and stay positive. Sometimes, it's hard not to dwell on the lengths people go to in order to spread the seeds of division and hatred, especially when what they are reacting to is a simple message of hope. But then I remember that some of them are misguided. Some of them haven't broadened their minds to think outside their immediate social circle or taken the time to think about what another person's life might be like. Some haven't had the education that I've had and have been drawn in by cheap slogans and propaganda. And some of them haven't accepted that times change and that our diversity, tolerance and empathy will make us grow as a society.

Shortly after I was elected lord mayor, a woman called Lisa wrote a lovely letter to *The Star*, one of our last remaining daily papers in Sheffield. Lisa and I had met at a function and she had taken it upon herself to write a message wishing me well, hoping that I would 'not only be a breath of fresh air, but a beacon of hope that unites us all'. Lisa encouraged me to 'bring a radical approach to the role, as well as celebrating all that is great about our wonderful city, [engaging] with all the hard-to-reach communities'. To be honest, even though it was a daunting task, I hoped for the same things.

However, in response to Lisa, a man named Paul Wake wrote the following letter, which was printed in *The Star* on 31 May 2018:

> I have been living in Sheffield for all my life (71 years), worked for a charity most of my life, paid my taxes and couldn't disagree with you more. This once great city that was famous for its world-class steel, home to the oldest football club and great history, is sadly changing. Sheffield is rapidly losing its identity and we must do something to stop it.
>
> I honestly believe Magid represents everything that is going wrong with our once great city and country. I'm sure I'm not alone when I say that such an esteemed role such as the

Lord Mayor (First Citizen) of Sheffield should only be reserved to a person of white English descent and especially not a Muslin immigrant, because that is our tradition and culture which is unfortunately slowly being eradicated.

We don't want a radical approach, we want and need an English approach. I just want the good old days back where we put English people first and this Magid bloke is going to ruin everything. Is that too much to ask for?

Paul Wake, S4

My immediate thoughts were drawn to thinking of the 'good old days', meaning the time when there were not many people of colour in Britain. The 'good old days' when women weren't allowed to vote and cholera was prevalent. The 'good old days' when it was ok to be a flagrant racist in public and no one would say anything back. But I chose to wait, and responded in a measured and less raw tone:

The past few days have honestly been overwhelming to say the least. I have been inundated with heartfelt kind messages of love and hope from all over the world that just fill me with such gratitude. And the fact that the media and people from across the globe have been talking about Sheffield in such a positive light fills me with pride.

However, it hasn't gone unnoticed that I have also sadly received messages and comments filled with nothing but hate and racism.

Believe it or not, I'm not here to cause trouble like one of the letters states. Neither am I here to change the world. I am here to champion and celebrate all that is great about our city, while bringing my own flavour to the role with the hope of engaging with a wider audience. In that process, if someone that I engage with, shake hands with or just share stories with happens to change our lives for the better, and if I can play any part in sparking that, it'll be a job well done.

You may not like it, but I am who I am because of this city. I have achieved what I have achieved because of this city and I am lord mayor because the people of this city (our city) have chosen me as their lord mayor.

I'm merely a reflection of this city which for the vast majority thankfully doesn't agree with you and is proud to do things differently. Me becoming lord mayor is as much of a celebration about the people of Sheffield as it is about me, as it hadn't been for the love, the compassion and the courage this city showed me, this story would have not been told. Thank you, Sheffield!

Magid

One thing people didn't know at the time was that the editor of *The Star*, conscious of not wanting to give a platform to racism, had asked me whether I thought they should publish Mr Wake's letter. At first I felt indifferent about it, but the more I thought about it, the more I felt that publishing it would present an opportunity for such views to be challenged. So I replied to say that I thought it should be made available for all to see.

I was ready. I wanted to show everyone what confronting and defeating the bigots looked like. While I didn't follow Michelle Obama's famous advice, 'When they go low, we go high', I opted for the British anti-fascist tradition of meeting racism and hatred head-on by calling it out. Because here is the thing: if Mr Wake had the audacity to write into our most widely circulated local newspaper without a hint of discomfort, how many other people thought the same as him?

Too many, to be sure. Answering them was important. But more than that, I wanted to show that I was not afraid, that I was willing to stand up and be counted because I represented so many other people in Sheffield who Mr Wake would consider 'not Sheffield enough', 'not English enough' – basically, not white enough. I knew that someone in a visible role had to say, 'Fuck that!' And besides, I knew how many white British people in Sheffield supported me, were excited to be represented by me and had helped me every step of the way.

I think sometimes it is important to show the underbelly of the world we are living in and call out prickish behaviour. Frankly, it is easier to do this when you're pretty sure that the majority is on your side. In Sheffield, I knew I was safe.

Mr Wake's letter may have been the first of its kind in my year as lord mayor, but it was far from the last. During my time in office, I kept a 'hate box' in the corner of the parlour (the fancy name for the lord mayor's office at the town hall) and filled it with dozens of abusive and hateful letters that I regularly received. But the online abuse was often worse, like when the far-right, Islamophobic English Defence League created a page for people to post messages of hate about me. This is sadly normal behaviour for them, as they always spew out hate based on the colour of people's skin, religion or the clothes people choose to wear to express themselves. As well as being a dangerously bigoted group, it is fair to say that they are firmly in the 'prick' category.

Several people wrote in to express their disgust about the Christmas jumper I wore while carrying a Christmas tree from the town hall to a volunteer-run café that served the vulnerable and the elderly. The jumper featured the words 'Jesus was a refugee'. One of the messages I received about it, from a man called Neil James, really got me going, in part because it was vile, but also because it was plain wrong:

> Why did the mayor insult the Christian prophet and son of God by wearing a 'Jesus was a refugee' T-shirt? Jesus wasn't a refugee and I'm offended that a Muslim, belonging to a highly sensitive and easily offended religion, had the audacity and pure

hatred in his heart to ridicule the son of God. If I wore a T-shirt that said 'Mohammed was a . . .', you and your brethren would be claiming offence and discrimination.

If you can't bear your prophet and religion being ridiculed and criticised, keep your nose out of the UK's religion, Christianity. This is a Christian country. Show some damned respect.

Jesus definitely was a refugee. How do I know? Well, it says so in the Bible with the story of the flight into Egypt in the Gospel of Matthew 2:13–14:

When they had gone, an angel of the Lord appeared to Joseph in a dream. 'Get up,' he said, 'take the child and his mother and escape to Egypt. Stay there until I tell you, for Herod is going to search for the child to kill him.' So he got up, took the child and his mother during the night and left for Egypt.

Jesus' entire family was forced to escape to a foreign country to secure their safety because King Herod intended to murder Jesus – they fled their homeland because they feared persecution. The

UN High Commissioner for Refugees defines a refugee as 'someone who has been forced to flee his or her country because of persecution, war or violence'. I suppose a crucial piece of advice I'd give to those seeking to avoid being unnecessarily mean is to do a little research to support your opinion – don't be arrogant in assuming you know more than someone else when you don't have the full facts. The whole point of the slogan was to encourage people to think about things differently. I'd wondered if people would have more sympathy for the plight of refugees if they remembered that Jesus was one, too.

I try to focus and appreciate the positive things in life rather than the pricks who are out to make life difficult for me, but I know that's easier said than done. I don't know who came up with 'Sticks and stones may break my bones, but words shall never hurt me,' but it's nonsense – words can sometimes hurt a lot more than broken bones. Just think of the irreparable pain of someone you love telling you that they don't love you anymore. Sometimes words break things inside us that we didn't even know could be broken. So how do we avoid this? It's simple – don't be a prick. Don't be arrogant.

And remember that whoever you are talking to has a life, feelings and stuff going on that you don't know about. People deserve compassion and kindness, even if you disagree with them. Being spiteful or treating someone with disdain will make them feel bad, but often it won't just end with them – it could affect their day and the people they interact with, and before you know it that negativity has spread far and wide. Your actions can affect people much more than you know, so why not try to have a positive impact?

It didn't break my heart, but one incident did almost make me lose my faith in humanity. It was a letter I received near the end of my term, from someone who was clearly still upset about my actions towards Donald Trump. On 4 July 2018, in advance of Trump's visit to the UK, I wore a T-shirt emblazoned with the words 'Donald Trump is a wasteman' and a sombrero, before walking to the monthly council meeting in Sheffield Town Hall. I also sent this tweet:

> I Magid Magid, lord mayor & first citizen of this
> city, hereby declare that not only is Donald J.
> Trump (@realDonaldTrump) a WASTEMAN,

but he is also henceforth banned from the great city of Sheffield!

I further declare 13 July to be Mexico Solidarity Day!

I chose 'wasteman' partly because it was the first thing that came into my head but also because, let's be honest, it's the least you can call Trump. Although it was a term that my friends and many people across the country used, I knew it wasn't familiar to broadcasters or to the vast majority of people aged 40 or above – I suspected and hoped that it would become a talking point and raise awareness. Was Trump ever going to visit Sheffield? Probably not, but telling him that he wasn't welcome in our great city was a symbolic gesture. I also listed five reasons (out of thousands I could have mentioned!) why he was a wasteman and five things that we can all do to beat him. The sombrero was given to me by the Mexican community in Sheffield who, on my invitation, attended the council meeting to perform traditional Mexican dances. Wearing it was my way of expressing solidarity with their country at a time when migrant children were being separated from their families at the US–Mexico border. Here's a letter that I received in response:

MAJiq THE MONKEY
You AREN'T WORTHY
to SUCK THE SHit out of
TRUMP'S ASS.
You ARE A NIGGER!
YOUR APE PARENTS ARE
NIGGERS!
FUCK YOU FAGGOT!
EAT SHit AND DiE!
xx JO COX

How can I begin to explain everything that's wrong with this letter? The vile racist language, the disgusting homophobia and the threat of harm, not to mention the sinister reference to a great woman who was brutally assassinated by a far-right terrorist.

When I received the letter, I decided to share it on Twitter – not to ask for sympathy or anger, but so it would to serve as a harsh reminder of the hate and intolerance that has penetrated to the very heart of our communities. A reminder of the difficulties we face in our struggle to build a fairer and more equal society. But I also put it out there as a call to arms, to let people know that we can, and will, continue in our struggle. We will continue to speak truth to power and won't let anybody scare us into silence. Yes, hate is pervasive and it causes real harm, but by embracing courage, compassion and hope we can defeat it. For the sake of humanity's future, we must defeat it. But to achieve that, we need each other.

* * *

One important way to defeat hate is to engage in conversations with people. These conversations aren't always easy but they can be a powerful tool for social change. I'm not saying that discussing Brexit with a xenophobic racist who believed Muslims were the root of all his problems was simple, but sometimes it's important to overcome barriers and gain a better understanding of each other. Stepping into other people's shoes, focusing on creating value and being compassionate are some techniques I've learned that have helped me. This applies to so many scenarios: in the classroom, in the pub, on Twitter or at a work appraisal.

The most important conversations you can have are with yourself. Who do you really want to be?

What is the change you want to see in the world? What price are you willing to pay for it to happen? And which enemies are you willing to make?

I have become more resistant to the abuse I get, but I think it helps that I'm always focused on something else. My energy is limited and it's always better to focus on the positive things and on the bigger objective. It's like the idea that when you're in a rush, you don't notice the rain. Just keep going – you might get wet, but a bit of water doesn't hurt. Honestly though, I also have a deep sense of pity for people who hate, and it's always worth remembering that you could be dealing with someone who is ill or hurting.

While I try to ignore anyone who throws any hate at me and encourage others to do the same, there are some instances when it might be worth engaging. If you're getting some hate from your Uncle Cyril or Lisa from down the road, or from someone who has genuine concerns or criticisms, it can be useful to listen to them, going the Michelle Obama route and taking the high road. Killing with kindness is a cliché for a reason: it can really work!

As a way to understand some of my naysayers and to show them that we had more in common than the things that divided us, I asked to meet some of the people who regularly sent negative letters about me to *The Star*. In a meeting organised by the paper, three of them came along. In all honesty, what I was expecting to be a fiery encounter was actually very positive. I don't know if it was the cupcakes that were provided or seeing me in the flesh, but it was not at all like the encounter I thought we would have. What I learned was that people who say things about you online never have the same energy when you're face-to-face with them – sometimes, although not always, they can be much kinder. Did we agree on everything? No. Did I win some of them over? Yes. Do some of them still think I'm a prick? Also yes.

Despite our differences, whether they be political, social or whether I should wear a suit or not, it is important to remember that I have more in common than not with the three people that came to the meeting. We all have to have a commitment to truth seeking and understand that truth seeking is not something you can do in a close-minded, self-righteous way. It requires values of intellectual humility and open mindedness. It means being willing to engage with others, willing to listen, willing to consider you're sometimes wrong, understanding that you're fallible, and understanding that truth-seeking is a joint process. Even when you're in an intense debate with a fellow truth-seeker, whatever your differences are, you've both got something more fundamental than those differences which is driving you: a desire to get to the truth of the matter.

Those same values are necessary to support a democracy. In a democracy fellow citizens are going to disagree about things, but they need to be bound together by principles, including principles about how we go about disagreeing with each other. This must be done respectfully and civilly, with the understanding that the other person is not an enemy to be defeated but rather a friend who is with you in the truth-seeking process and also looking for the common good, even though you might reach different conclusions.

You might reach different conclusions on whether Brexit is good for the country or a disaster, whether the royal family should be abolished or not, or if people who voluntarily wear crocs need to seek help or not. You can disagree about those things. The key is that when you disagree about those things, in order to sustain this democracy, you have to understand that we have to respect each other, be willing to listen to each other and most importantly be willing to learn from each other.

Some time later, on my first day at work as an MEP, I had a less positive face-to-face encounter. Imagine: it's your first day at your new job and you're probably excited and nervous. You're looking forward to getting to know some new people and exploring this new place you're going to call home for a bit. The last thing you expect is to be made to feel uncomfortable and then to have some arrogant prick come up to you, asking, 'Are you lost?' before telling you to leave the building.

I was initially baffled and confused, but then I quickly became annoyed. However, I decided not to call it out as racism – I wanted to know more about the motivations behind their simple words. I'd like to think it was a misunderstanding, maybe something to do with my dress sense being unusual for the European Parliament, and nothing more – until I saw other MEPs also wearing t-shirts with slogans. And yet, the incident is all too familiar for many black and minority ethnic people, especially those excelling in any field: our clothes are scrutinised, our appearance is criticised, our non-conformism is ridiculed and our mere presence is questioned.

DON'T BE A PRICK

Sometimes people don't know how to communicate well, so it can be a challenge to tell the Uncle Cyrils and the Lisas from the Mr Wakes and the Mr Richardsons. That's when reaching out to people who you know are on your side is most important. If you need support or help, contact friends or share the problem with allies. And if you feel in danger, contact the police or the security team at your school or place of work. Hate breeds in secrecy, so you can take it away from those hateful people by shining a light on it.

Remember that making change in the world requires functioning organisations and movements, and these are always collective efforts. The winning formulas all have common elements: a successful, efficient team and a support mechanism. They may look like cogs in a well-oiled machine from the outside, but from the inside you can see that they are built on friendship and mutual positive regard. No one is being a prick, and that is how we can help one another and work to combat hatred.

III
DO EPIC SHIT

'I'm not saying I'm going to rule the world or I'm going to change the world. But I guarantee that I will spark the brain that will change the world. That's our job — to spark somebody else watching us.'

Tupac Shakur

This chapter isn't just here to allow me to show off about the things that have happened in my life. Claiming that anything I've done is 'epic' isn't my style – it just makes me feel uncomfortable. I've been bold, I've said 'yes' to a lot of things and I've taken risks, and I'm definitely proud of that. The other really important thing is to say is that only some of these risks have paid off and I'm going to talk here about both the successes and the failures, and what I've learned from them. Taking risks, whatever the outcome, is what makes us grow most of all.

I get asked how I got into politics quite a lot, and I notice that people often seem scared of that word. It conjures up a vision of an old white guy a long way away in a fancy building with columns making decisions that seem to make ordinary people's lives a little bit worse. Other people feel so detached and disengaged from the system that they don't realise they have the power to change it. I sometimes joke around when people ask me how I got into politics, but when I tell them what actually happened, I can see that they start to think, 'Huh – maybe I could be a politician too.' People don't know how to go about it, so I try to inform them how they can. We all have it in our power to do something epic – we just need to have the courage to get out there and help other people.

It feels like this entire politics thing is a bit of an adventure – the sort of adventure where you face barriers along the way but know you're working towards a bigger positive goal. I've never really had much of a career plan: I studied aquatic zoology at Hull University, founded a start-up business, worked for the housing charity Shelter, got elected as a councillor, became Lord Mayor of Sheffield and was then elected an MEP. It hasn't exactly been a traditional career path! Along the way, I've always found myself thinking, 'Where am I going next – what's the next expedition going to be?'

I try to look through the prism of adventure in everything I do, but the desire to make a positive contribution is always bubbling away too. I suppose I've always had a desire to take risks, a feeling that I want to step out of my comfort zone and experience new things. Wondering what might happen, what you might discover, who you might meet and what change you can make is what I live for – being uncomfortable is where the magic happens.

Everything worthwhile I've ever achieved has started with an element of fear and discomfort – I've even started to use it as a barometer. The more scared and nervous something makes me feel (within reason, of course!), the more I push myself to do it – it's become a familiar feeling that I acknowledge and welcome. Let's face it, it's fear that keeps us alive, and it should never stop us from doing what matters.

*   *   *

I grew up imagining epic journeys in my mind, but had no idea how to go about making them. Then the internet supplied me with all the information I needed to put something I'd dreamed about into reality – it was my single most important influence during my teenage years. I'll never forget the day we got the internet. My mum had put all her savings into buying us a computer from PC World. It was the size of a small shed and took two people to lift it, and I could just tell that it was going to change everything.

I developed a fascination with travel websites that verged on the obsessive. The photos of these amazing destinations, from Machu Picchu in Peru and Mount Kilimanjaro in Tanzania to Chichen Itza in Mexico, made me want to visit so many places. Then I found out that you could get travel brochures that had the most incredible photos for free, so I ordered a shitload. My mum must have thought something dodgy was going on because I was spending all my time on the internet and then, out of nowhere, I started receiving a lot of post. In reality, I was looking at pictures of mountains in far-off lands and dreaming of the day I would leave Burngreave and see the world.

Mountains have always fascinated me. Perhaps it's because they signify adventure, inviting me to conquer something and better myself along the way, but they also showed me that there was more to the world than I already knew. They spoke to my natural curiosity and appealed to the satisfaction I gained from doing something worthwhile. However, I didn't know how bloody expensive it was to go on any of these trips, especially to some of the mountains I dreamed of climbing.

I started reading a lot of travel blogs and thinking of unusual ways I might be able pay the ridiculous prices to go on exotic climbing expeditions, but there was no way around it. That being said, I refused to let the cost put me off – I just figured I'd need a while to save up. So I got a job at the Next distribution centre in Wath upon Dearne, working 12-hour shifts every day. Although I was doing some of the most mind-numbing work I've ever done, there were some really weird and wonderful people that made working there bearable.

Once I'd got enough cash together, I went on a three-week alpine mountaineering course in the Swiss Alps. Walking around in crampons, wielding an ice axe and learning about crevasse rescue felt quite surreal, not to mention nerve-wracking. The highest peak we climbed was Weissmies, a 4,017-metre peak in the south of Switzerland. There were times we were literally walking on clouds and I was thinking, 'Shouldn't I be in a plane right now?'

The alpine mountaineering course was where my ambition to climb the 'Seven Summits' – the highest mountains on each continent – started. The first on my list was Kilimanjaro in Tanzania. I'd always wanted to climb 'Kili' – it used to be on the front of so many travel brochures, with its flat, snow-capped peak rising majestically above the savannah and a bunch of giraffes munching away in the foreground. When most people are planning to climb one of the Seven Summits, they go through agencies and pay various fees, but I couldn't afford that. Despite all the hours I'd worked, I still hadn't saved enough to do it the conventional way, so I researched what exactly the operator did and figured out how to do it myself.

I booked a flight to Kilimanjaro International Airport and took a bus to the nearest town, Moshi, on the lower slopes of the mountain. My plan was to find someone who had climbed Kili before (I reckoned there would be loads of them) and ask him or her if we could climb it together – I figured that would be the cheapest way to do it. So that's exactly what I did – I met as many people as possible and eventually found Mustafa, a local who'd done it before and was up for an adventure. And so off we went.

When we were a few days into the climb, my biggest fear became a reality and I started to suffer from altitude sickness. The thing with getting this condition during an expedition is that, (a) it's horrible and (b) it can really ruin your chances of reaching the top. I could have bought some medication called Diamox before I set off, but I remember it being really expensive and I'd just assumed that everything would have been fine. Boy, was I wrong! People react to altitude sickness in different ways, but if it's not treated it can become life-threatening. I remember becoming nauseous, vomiting and feeling breathless.

Having no choice but to stop the ascent and climb down slightly to a lower altitude (the main treatment for altitude sickness), I could tell that Mustafa was

worried – and this was someone who'd been climbing this mountain longer than I'd been alive! Fortu-
nately, while I was vomiting next to some secluded
rocks not far from my tent, I met two Dutch ladies
who saw me struggling and offered me some large,
bullet-shaped pills. Though I was not entirely sure
what I'd been given, I ripped one out of its foil wrap-
ping and held it in my hand, preparing to swallow it.
But then the Dutch ladies started frantically gesticu-
lating that the pill needed to go *up the other end*. The
gestures they used to explain the process will stay
with me forever . . .

I trudged to the nearest rock I could hide behind,
contemplating how I'd ended up on the world's highest free-standing mountain, feeling sick and about to
shove a pre-lubed suppository up my rear end. It was
not exactly how I'd imagined I was going to conquer
Mount Kilimanjaro, with two Dutch ladies and my
new friend Mustafa chanting, 'You can do it, Magid!'
Just the moral support I needed.

After hesitating for several minutes, I finally did
it – the thought of not completing the climb was
more unbearable than the suppository. Thankfully, it
did the job, getting rid of the nausea and enabling
me to reach the summit, so I'm massively grateful

to those two awesome Dutch Samaritans. What the experience taught me, apart from what a suppository is, was that it's not the end of the world if you haven't got the resources you need – you've just got to think creatively to get round obstacles in your path. As a result, I met some amazing people and had some experiences I wouldn't have had otherwise, and I feel like I'm a better person for it. I hadn't let logistics stand in the way of my dreams, and the struggle had made the whole thing more epic.

*   *   *

I adopted the same approach when I was in the Amazon, another place I'd always wanted to go to. I think Brazil had always appealed to me – not just because I'd spent years grappling with opponents in Brazilian jiu-jitsu but because I had a fascination with the Amazon and its indigenous communities. This was the trip where I had my first experience of couch-surfing after a friend told me about it. It's like Airbnb, but free – it's basically a homestay and social networking service that allows you to host people from around the world or to stay with locals in their own homes. It's based on the idea that people are generally kind and it's a fantastic way to meet and learn from people all over the world. My hosts were a gay couple who picked me up from Galeão International Airport in Rio, introduced me to their family and then put me up with one of their cousins in a favela called Vidigal. The two and a half months I spent there showed me that, contrary to popular belief, it was a safer place than downtown Rio, with a strong sense of community.

I couldn't have travelled all this way to Brazil without attempting to visit some of the indigenous Amazonian tribes while I was there. I found out that excursions to meet tribespeople were organised through a government agency called Fundação Nacional do Índio (or Funai), which protects the interests and culture of indigenous communities. Again though, this would have required some hefty fees and I just simply didn't have the money. But what I did have was the will to do whatever it took to find a solution. So what I did might sound familiar: I went to the nearest large town. It was a place called Altamira, where the government had just approved the construction of the hugely controversial Belo Monte Dam, a colossal hydroelectric project that would lead to 500 square kilometres of land being flooded and thousands of indigenous people being displaced, not to mention the threat to wildlife.

Altamira is located at the mouth of the Xingu River, a tributary of the Amazon where the Xingu peoples are based. The region is occupied by 15 tribes who speak eight different languages but share many beliefs and practices. I was desperate to get there, so I went out and met as many people as possible, to try and find out how I might be able to get round the official channel. One day I met Miriam, who as luck had it worked for a branch of Funai. She was Guyanese and offered to introduce me to some of the Xingu peoples. She told me that I should show them a bit of gratitude, so I took sugar, tobacco and textbooks with me. After a 15-hour boat journey up the Xingu River, I spent two weeks with one of the tribes. I communicated mainly through body language but could tell that they appreciated the gifts I'd brought with me. I spent most of my time helping them build nets for fishing, eating some amazing fruit and swimming in beautiful crystal-clear water that was a long way from the piranha-infested murky swamp you see in Hollywood depictions of the Amazon.

The time I spent with the welcoming and kind Xingu tribes influenced the way I approached my later work in the European Parliament, when I worked with migrants and helped to protect the rights of minority communities, whose continued existence is often under threat. The Xingu peoples work hard to preserve the environment, preventing illegal loggers, ranchers and gold miners from damaging their sacred landscape, some of which includes protected national parks. They have a remarkable culture, but the construction of the Belo Monte Dam threatens to displace entire communities and alter the balance of the delicate ecosystem in the planet's most treasured rainforest.

The journey back to Altamira was tricky. I kept on catching rides up-river, getting dropped somewhere and having to wait a few hours for the next boat to pass. It took some time but I eventually I got back to Altamira. Looking back on it now, I realise I was completely reckless during this trip. My family had no idea where I was and I hadn't worried about vaccinations or malaria tablets – I think I was just consumed by a thirst for adventure. I figured that I just had to put my faith in the world and think, 'This is the only option I've got, so what have I got to lose?'

As much as I carefully listen to my gut feelings, I always give people I meet and situations I find myself in the benefit of the doubt. If I didn't see the best in people and was always on guard, I think I'd probably have a shit time – everything I'd do wouldn't be as fun or liberating. I genuinely believe that only a tiny minority of people want to do others harm, and the best experiences I've had have involved putting my faith in people. Like staying on random people's couches – anything can happen. I used to host a lot of people, and would still do it now – it's much better than staying in a hotel, because you actually get to meet local people and exchange stories. And when you meet lots of new people, it always leads on to other things. People are generally really proud to show you what they love, and seeing what other people are passionate about helps you discover hidden gems that there's no way you'd have found out about otherwise. You want to have that kind of authenticity when you're travelling. During my adventure in Brazil, I hung out with some of the best people I've ever met, ate some of the best food I've ever had and had a completely unique experience. I'm proud to still call those people friends today.

There are many places I still want to go to, particularly those places that may still be untainted by society's ills and are so different to anything I've seen before. I used to really want to climb Everest, and to be frank I still do, but we're talking tens of thousands of pounds, even if you use a local Nepali company, and there's no enterprising way to get around that! In 2017, a South African guy who attempted to reach the summit without a permit was arrested and fined $22,000. I'd also need to climb another of the eight-thousanders (the 8,000-metre peaks) to help me acclimatise to the altitude. Most people seem to choose Cho Oyu on the China–Nepal border – it's the one Edmund Hillary climbed in 1952, as preparation for the first successful attempt at Everest. But then I consider what the real cost of climbing Everest would be. Would it be to the detriment of the local community and the sherpas? I remember reading that 11 tonnes of rubbish were cleared from the overcrowded slopes last year and it makes me think twice. It's always has to be a balance between wanting to do something for yourself and wanting to help others.

* * *

'Doing epic shit' can be a tiny thing that helps you grow, helps someone else or even sets off a chain reaction that leads to something great. Soon after I was elected Lord Mayor of Sheffield, a Somali girl in her twenties from Belgium wrote to me on Instagram to say that I'd inspired her to get involved in politics – she was thinking about running as a local councillor. She asked for my advice and I wrote back with some thoughts and words of encouragement. Thanks in part to something that I'd done, she went on to do some epic shit herself! The act of giving advice to someone who goes on to achieve something they're proud of means a lot to me. In a famous interview with MTV in 1994, the rapper Tupac Shakur said: 'I'm not saying I'm going to rule the world or I'm going to change the world. But I guarantee that I will spark the brain that will change the world. That's our job – to spark somebody else watching us.'

Inspiring others matters far more to me than personal glory, because it lasts. I've been fortunate that since I've been involved in politics, I've been in a position to help people who need it, but small acts of kindness can also inspire others to follow your example.

When I was a local councillor in Sheffield, my mum told me about a Somali friend of hers who'd received a frightening-looking eviction notice. She rented the flat where she lived with her three kids, and it turned out that she'd amassed rent arrears because her English wasn't good enough to be able to fill out a form notifying the authorities of a change in her status. I knew I could help her – I spoke Somali and could interpret for her, but she also needed the emotional support. So I went with her to help explain to the council what had happened. We waited for an hour and a half for a council officer to appear, during which time she regaled me with stories about life in Somalia before the civil war before changing tack and offering me some earnest (and slightly unnecessary!) marriage advice. The face-to-face conversation with the council officer sorted the problem, and while it didn't take that much time out of my day, the impact on her family was huge. It made me realise that we sometimes find that we have the ability to help someone in need, even if we don't know it – if everyone performed a random act of kindness like this, I think it would change the world.

Helping out this lady was just one of those times when supplying information to someone who didn't know where to find it made all the difference. I've done this countless times for young people who aren't aware of their rights or of the free services they can access. I quickly realised that young people seem to relate to me – I guess it's because I don't look like your average politician and because I speak to them sincerely. Seeing someone that looks like them or that they can relate to makes such a difference – it's one of the many reasons why representation is so important. It is incredibly empowering for a young person or a member of a minority community to see someone who looks and talks like them in a position of influence. Still, it is very important that we don't make the mistake of subscribing to trickle-down identity politics. Simply more black or brown faces in high places will not solve deep-rooted issues for anybody.

One thing that really does make me anxious and scared is public speaking, but having the role I do, it's not something I can avoid. Every time I'm about to walk out, although I look cool, calm and collected, I promise you that my heart races and I get sweaty palms. Don't get me wrong, I'm fine if it's just a few words, anything formal and more than 5 minutes long is tough for me. Regardless of how much I practice, when it comes to it, I'm still absolutely bricking it. There have also been times when I've not prepared for a speech but have forced myself to get out there and speak, while telling myself that if it goes badly I'll only have myself to blame for putting myself in that situation. I know it sounds weird, but at times like this

I feel like I just need to take responsibility for allowing myself to be so unprepared in that situation. That being said, there hasn't ever been a time where I've regretted facing my fears and stepping up to the lectern – overcoming the fear is a crucial way to learn, develop and achieve something great. Planning and practicing always helps, too.

When people ask me about things I've done, I prefer to talk about the fact that regardless of background and ability, we are all capable of doing amazing things. All it takes is believing in yourself, taking risks and not asking for permission, but making sure you ask for help if you need it. One teenage girl who has stood up for what she believes in and asked others to join her has changed the world: Greta Thunberg skipped school one day to protest outside the Swedish Parliament building by herself, holding a simple sign that read 'Skolstrejk för klimatet' – school strike for the climate. Sometimes it takes just one person to voice a point that many are thinking but don't have the courage to do anything about. I guess people always look to others to sort something out instead of asking themselves, 'If not me, then who?' Rather than just hoping something will change, try taking action yourself. It doesn't have to be something you do specifically for other people – it might just be for yourself. Even empowering yourself can have an inspiring effect on other people.

Fear keeps us from doing epic shit, but you can overcome it. When people ask me what I'm afraid of, I think of unfulfilled ambition and not pushing myself far enough. And I know that sounds a bit like an answer from a job interview, but it's the truth. I try to remind myself that my mother didn't come this far and make all the sacrifices she did for me not to achieve my potential. I know that she's proud of me, and that keeps me moving forward.

When fear is holding me back from achieving something I really want to do, I'm reminded of the following quote from Teddy Roosevelt that encourages me to put myself out there:

> It is not the critic who counts; not the man who points out how the strong man stumbles, or where the doer of deeds could have done them better. The credit belongs to the man who is actually in the arena, whose face is marred by dust and sweat and blood; who strives valiantly; who errs, who comes short again and again, because there is no effort without error and shortcoming; but who

does actually strive to do the deeds; who knows great enthusiasms, the great devotions; who spends himself in a worthy cause; who at the best knows in the end the triumph of high achievement, and who at the worst, if he fails, at least fails while daring greatly, so that his place shall never be with those cold and timid souls who neither know victory nor defeat.[1]

These words remind me to be bold, to embrace being uncomfortable and to take risks. Whenever I've decided on a project or am making a tough decision, like deciding to stand as to be lord mayor, I try to be bold and go all in – in my experience, there's nothing worse than the feeling of regret that you could have given more and wondering 'what if'. Don't have a half-arsed attitude, don't procrastinate and try to stay focused.

Being bold means following through on an idea or a dream and giving it your best shot, always making

---

[1] Part of Teddy Roosevelt's 'Citizenship in a Republic' speech which came to be known as 'The Man in the Arena', given in Paris, 23 April 1910

sure that your contribution is meaningful and effective. I've found that there are too many things you can't control for you to compromise on your efforts and not exhaust the full extent of your ability. Being bold means grabbing opportunities with both hands and not letting go until you've done them justice, regardless of the outcome.

I've always felt that whenever something could go either way the best policy is to take a deep breath and go for it – and if the odds are better than that, you have no excuse! Too many people are scared of losing, which can stifle their potential to have an impact. Everyone loses at some point – no great person hasn't, whether in politics, business or life. But you'll win when it matters, and when you do, things will open up in your life that you could never have dreamed of. Build up the courage to step out of your comfort zone and into a place where you may feel insecure or maybe even unworthy. This is where you will most definitely grow, and it is a place where epic shit is possible.

IV
SEE THE GOOD

'Darkness cannot drive out darkness; only light can do that.
Hate cannot drive out hate; only love can do that.'
Martin Luther King

'See the good' seems like a simple enough instruction, but when you ask people what they think it means, they'll probably come up with different answers. They might talk about thinking positively, using empathy to see the good in other people or seeing the possibility in every situation. They might talk about happy memories of their past, or they may think about the positive impact we can play in other people's lives. And all these responses are things I want to talk about, because they add up to something special. 'See the good' can mean many different things – all of them based on seeing positivity and light in life.

I'm going to start where I did – with my mum. There are lots of traits and qualities I think I take from her – kindness, ambition, positivity and hopefulness – even if it's slightly misplaced, like the time she insisted that she could grow an avocado in our back garden in Sheffield. All these things help me see the good and keep coming back to it, whatever the context.

My favourite characteristic that I've inherited from my mum is her smile. She's always smiling, and every time I see a picture of me smiling, I think of her. There are some things we don't agree on though, and we have very different visions of what

93

success is. For her, having gone through numerous hardships and sacrificed so much, success is stability. That means having a secure job that pays well, so you can look after the people you love. To her, success also means finding a loving wife and raising loving children. She worries about me and wonders if I'm ever going to find someone to share my life with or get a permanent job. Every parent wants the best for their children and I know that's true of my mum too. Even though we are poles apart on some things, she's the most important person in my life.

* * *

My life recently has been somewhat unpredictable. All my correspondence goes to my mum's house, even though I haven't lived there for a while – maybe I'm not ready to call somewhere else home yet. Maybe having my post sent to her house is a good thing because it means that I go back there regularly – when I throw myself into work, it can be some time before I emerge. She knows that I get stressed doing what I do and is always saying, 'Stop working so hard – you need to look after yourself.' I always tell her I'm fine, but I'm not sure she's convinced. And she always makes sure that I recharge so that I'm able to see the good in people and keep going.

My unpredictable life has led me to always be hopeful and positive, which I find attracts other positive people. When I look back, whether at relationships, work, friends or my travels, I tend to only think of the happy memories. I can't help but think of all the sweet stuff, the good things – maybe that's my way of reinforcing a kind of positivity cycle. It means that no matter what comes my way, I'm ready to face it with a smile.

I think this positive attitude has helped me in the last few years in politics as a local councillor, lord mayor and MEP. When you're a councillor, the work never stops. People would often call me at the weekend or in the evening to ask questions and sometimes I had no idea what to do, but I'd make sure I found out, even if it took me some time. I might need to ring people I know, like a friend from university who's now a solicitor for legal advice, or I'd watch a YouTube tutorial on how to fix a leaky tap, but I'd get there. During my two years as a councillor, every day was a new day and I'd never know what the next one was going to hold. I'd face different challenges but I'd get to help people that needed it and to learn more about myself, which always puts a smile on my face.

As a cabinet member or senior MP, you might spend your time talking about big ideas like fiscal policy, but it's hard to see the effects of what you're working on day-to-day because you're not at the business end. By contrast, as a councillor you're much more connected with what's going on in the area you represent. For example (I say 'for example' as if this is just hypothetical, but all my examples tend to be real . . .) you might be contacted by a lady who, through no fault of her own, has had her Personal Independence Payment (a benefit that helps with the cost of a long-term health condition or disability) cut. I found fixing problems like this hugely rewarding, as I could see the effect I was having and how much it meant. Sometimes the good you can do for someone can be life-changing, especially when you're the last line of defence before they end up at a foodbank or living on the street.

A lot of people don't know where to go to when they have an issue in their community that they want sorted – part of the problem is that they don't know what politicians and councillors actually do, and I can't blame them for that. I don't remember being taught about it at school or receiving any helpful information through the letterbox. So when I became a councillor, I thought to myself, 'If I can make myself as visible as possible and tell people I can help address local issues they have, maybe I can make a real difference in my community.' I would attend as many community events as I could, even if I didn't get an invitation – I would always cheerfully show up, no matter what. I also put my email and phone number on my leaflets, inviting people to call or email me – I wanted to make it easier for them. Not everyone can turn up at a community surgery on the second Tuesday of every month between 2pm and 4pm, for example, especially if they're elderly, disabled or have young kids.

The problem with my new approach was that it was too effective – it got to a point where I was struggling with the number of emails, calls and on-the-spot enquiries I was receiving. This highlighted how many people needed help but didn't have the resources, time or knowledge to combat the local issues they were facing, which meant that I found myself getting really invested in people's problems. Being a councillor and representing the people in your ward is not the sort of job where you can just go home at 5pm. I've never been good at working specific hours, so it sort of suited me. I'd get in to work at 8am and leave at 9pm, but even then would always end up taking work home – but somehow, it just didn't feel like work.

I was struggling to cope with the workload at the beginning, as I was saying yes to everything and everyone. Being a councillor is a lot of things, but it's definitely not well paid. I got £933 a month for the two years I was a councillor – it's funny how that amount has stuck in my head! Even as lord mayor, I only got a top-up of £7,000. The crazy thing was that as part of the job I got a chauffeured car and was required to wear a massive gold chain,[2] so naturally people thought I was loaded!

Although I didn't have much money in the bank, I was happy and learned to live within my means. In my first year as a councillor, I'd found a bargain flatshare with a friend for £350, including bills. After buying food, my mobile phone and other living expenses, I was left with a good couple of hundred quid each month, but it was never enough to go on holiday abroad.

What I didn't realise at first was that the vast majority of councillors also had full-time jobs, though I

---

[2] The livery collar or chain of office that I was required to wear whenever I was in public representing the City of Sheffield.

couldn't see how that would be possible in a ward like Broomhill and Sharrow Vale, which included one of the most socially deprived areas in Sheffield as well as a large concentration of students. It was a fascinating, dynamic and exciting ward to repre- sent – I could have pulled back a bit and got a part- time job, but there was so much to do that it just wasn't feasible. Eventually, I asked Sheffield Hallam University for help, and they offered me a couple of keen interns who would work with me for 30 hours a week for two months, gaining practical experience that would count as part of their courses. I got some much-needed help and these guys gained some vital work experience .

One of the things that this taught me was the potential of win-win situations, where two groups could get things they needed – there's always room for more than one win. One complaint from some residents in my ward was that the students weren't actively engaged in the community, so I arranged for University of Sheffield law undergraduates to help elderly people with legal issues such as heating allowance payments, council tax support, pension credits and Personal Independence Payments. The help these students provided would benefit their CVs and gain them credits that counted towards their degrees, and at the same time, a bunch of elderly people's lives became a little bit easier. The third consequence, which in hindsight was possibly the most important, was that two different generations connected, learning a lot more about each other and often having a great time in the process. That can only be a good thing, especially at a time when the political chasm between generations is so stark.

Win-win situations can sometimes be a lot harder to come by, but that doesn't stop me trying. This hope that there might be a mutual path forward, at least in some areas, is part of the reason why I still smile at members of Identity and Democracy, a group of nationalist, populist and Eurosceptic parties from nine European nations, and hold the lift doors for them in the European Parliament. Maybe I'm trying to kill them with kindness, but I do hold a distinction between people who hold different views to me and those who take it to the next level by acting on the hate-fuelled rhetoric they hear.

A lot of the time, I think people's anger is misdirected. I'm not saying that you should just agree to disagree on things like racism – there's a time to fight fire with fire, and I always call racists out. And if someone's being beaten up because of their sexual orientation, I'm going to get involved and stand up for them. But at the same time, I'm a firm believer in having difficult conversations with people who hold views that are the polar opposite of your own and trying to find a way through. If we don't sit down and talk about it, everyone's just going to go back to their own echo chambers. In some cases, I'll realise that I'm wrong and they're right so I'll be enlightened, and that has to be a positive thing! Or maybe they'll come round to my side and my own beliefs will be reaffirmed. At the very least, it may lead to a sense of mutual understanding and perhaps even some empathy.

* * *

A guy called Ronni Abergel founded the Human Library with three friends in Copenhagen in 2000. It's a non-profit organisation that seeks to challenge stigma and stereotypes through dialogue – the idea is that, just like in a real library, you 'borrow' a human being and talk to them about things you would not normally talk about. The 'book' is typically someone who has experienced prejudice, social exclusion or stigma, and offers themselves up to questions, so that participants can hopefully re-examine their prejudices.

I volunteered for a Human Library Event at the Central Library in Sheffield, explaining that I was a Muslim, Somali-born migrant who had suffered prejudice. I was excited, as it felt like a great way to show the benefits of seeing the good in people and having a discussion with others, regardless of your differences. To my surprise, one 'reader' calmly said to me, 'I think all Muslims are evil – it's a religion that we should be eradicating rather than promoting, and that's just what I believe.' He went on to talk about Muslims being responsible for 9/11 and other atrocities. Although I found what he had to say difficult to hear, I was fascinated by what had caused him to believe what he did. We made some ground because by the end of our conversation he was able to conclude that not all Muslims are bad. Maybe in time, some of what I said might sink in and he'll challenge his own views. If I had just argued back and not listened or tried to see where his views came from, that would never have been possible.

Another aspect of seeing the good is making sure people can always see the good in me. This involves making myself as approachable as possible, particularly when I'm walking around Sheffield, and presenting myself as calm and open, even to people who disagree with me. I care and actually want to listen, whether or not we agree – if anything, I care even more when people disagree with me. Maybe that's because in those cases I want the opportunity to change their minds, but I also want to gain a better understanding of why people have arrived at the beliefs they have. Perhaps even more importantly than that, I want people to celebrate the things that unite them.

In the summer of 2016, as a newly elected local councillor, I was invited to speak at the Sheffield Black Lives Matter 'Peace Rally' on Devonshire Green, a small open space in the centre of the city. It had been organised by an amazing group of teenage activists, including a 16-year-old called Abdullah Mohammed, who eventually became a friend of mine. Like me, he came from the north of Sheffield, but unlike me, he stayed in the city for university and was later elected the President of Sheffield Hallam's Students' Union. On the day he took up his new role, Abdullah gave one of the most impassioned speeches I have ever witnessed. His message was simple: 'We need to stand together. No matter if you're white, black, ethnic or Russian – I don't care what you are. We need to come together, because despite our differences, we share the same struggle.' It was a simple but immensely powerful message about unity and seeing the good in everyone.

In politics, people sometimes look for the knock-down argument or the perfect soundbite, but in my experience the most powerful messages are those that are rooted in a fundamental feeling of compassion. Coming together and connecting is the first step to compassion, which is what defeats hate. But in order to foster compassion, you have to be willing to be vulnerable in public and to hope that others will see the good in you, which isn't easy. But Abdullah showed us how it can be done: by feeling deeply, and sharing that feeling, in broad daylight. I was so inspired by his positive message, moved by the impact his speech had on the crowd of students and hopeful about the next generation of young activists that I was prompted to write a letter to the young people of Sheffield, telling them how strongly I felt about the power they have and the importance of remembering to see the good:

I thought I'd write a little message to all young people. As my tenure as lord mayor draws closer to an end, I would have deeply regretted not writing directly to you.

Because let me tell you something — you are the hope shining through in a city, a country, a world largely and repeatedly failed by most of its influential adults.

Every school invitation, every selfie or cheery shout out on the street, every heartfelt message on social media. Whether you graced the Town Hall with your visits or if we stood shoulder to shoulder demanding urgent change, for the sake of your future and the future of our planet.

You should know that you are now and forever my real inspiration. You are my real fuel to keep fighting for a better world, without fear, without holding back. Your passion empowers us, and your sense of priorities and urgency keep us in check. I am, and will be eternally grateful.

I'm not a hero or perfect in any way. But I hope I've used this platform well enough to get you thinking more critically about politics, and how it affects everything and everyone!

I may not be lord mayor for much longer, but the battle to save the world will not end anytime soon.

If you agree, then be kind enough to pledge that you'll never forget these FIVE Cs:

— **Compassion**. This should be at the heart of everything we do. Don't let anybody ever tell you that it's weak to show emotion or to care. We are our strongest when we do care. And when we care, we are motivated to act, to fight fear with hope, to try to remedy injustices and to speak truth to power!

— **Courage**. Never let anybody tell you you're not good enough, not old or 'mature' enough, not smart enough. Challenge! Try! Don't be afraid to do things differently. Not only will you lead the way and break down barriers, but courage is contagious! You'll inspire everyone around you too!

— **Community**. We all aspire to live in a safer, fairer, more equal society. One that is diverse and yet inclusive, one that shares basic common values and yet is tolerant of others. We live in a world that's constantly trying to drive us apart — let's fight back, and work to bring people together!

SEE THE GOOD

— **Cope**. The world can be a beautiful place. Love, good company, delicious food, great music, the breath-taking countryside. But it isn't always like that. Things can get difficult, and painfully so. All we can do is try to adopt healthy coping mechanisms and always have each other's backs! Always!

— **Change**. Nothing you see in the system you were born into and are growing up in is natural. Someone decided things should be that way — never forget this. You are great enough to bring about the change you think is necessary, no matter how big, to make the world a better place!

That's a reminder for myself first and foremost, but I hope there's something in there for each of you.

From my end, I make a sincere pledge to fight by your side, to carry you with me wherever I go and in every decision I make, with your best interests at heart.

Yours lovingly forever and always,

The youngest-ever Lord Mayor of Sheffield

Magid x

If we aim to always see the good in others, we can change the world. If we look for the good despite our differences, or even just the possibility of good, it will enable us to have conversations and listen to other people's views. We can use our happy memories of the past to get us through tough times in the present and to remember that the world has good things to offer, no matter how hard the present feels. Within each and every one of us, there is the possibility to do good in our special ways. Seeing the good encourages others to do the same – optimism is contagious, after all. You may even start a chain reaction of positivity and kindness, and who knows how far this will go or which mind you might spark.

V
DON'T LOSE HOPE

'Do not judge me by my successes, judge me by how many times I fell down and got back up again.'
Nelson Mandela

Like everyone, I've experienced some really low points in my life, but one thought has always kept me going: the belief that a better life for me, my loved ones and others is possible. To put it frankly, the alternative sucks, which leaves me with no other option. In my early twenties, I was navigating an especially difficult period of my life and had no idea how to go about trying to help build a better world. Now, in my early thirties, I'm still learning.

After university, I was at my lowest ebb and was diagnosed with clinical depression, but two slightly surprising things picked me up when I didn't think it was possible. The first involved taking a chance on an advert, which changed everything, and the second was joining the Green Party and standing to be a councillor. I've learned that there is always hope, even in the most obscure places, and that the need for compassion in the way we do politics and life has never been greater. So never lose hope; you never know what's waiting around the corner, but you have to first believe that things can change and then have the courage to take steps towards this change.

* * *

After studying aquatic zoology at Hull University, a course I'd chosen partly after my mind had been blown by scuba diving in Zanzibar, I knew I didn't want to pursue a career in conservation or become a marine biologist. I ran a successful campaign and got elected as president of the students' union, but then I failed to get re-elected, which massively hit my confidence and left me in a tailspin. Not knowing what to do and what I wanted from the world, I decided to start a digital marketing business with two friends, with the support of the university's enterprise centre. After we had spent a year working on the venture, our visions for the company changed and we parted ways. I was left with no plans about what to do next. I was unemployed at a time when all my friends and family had high expectations of me. I was still living in Hull, while my closest friends had left to start their own adventures. I'd ended a relationship with the first girl I'd ever loved, and that hurt me in ways I never knew were possible. It all led me to a really dark place of feeling lonely, lost and depressed.

I didn't seek any support or help but just bottled everything up and decided that it was best to deal with it by myself. Reflecting on it now, I think I felt that it just wasn't socially acceptable to be vulnerable and express myself honestly – I know it's not healthy, but it's just how I've always dealt with things. So I just smiled and pretended that everything was ok, while secretly feeling completely worthless and guilty. I also wasn't eating properly, which made everything feel even worse.

I didn't know what to do, so I went to the Jobcentre in Hull to sign on. I still remember walking in there for the first time, nervously keeping my head down and praying that no one would see me because of the stigma that's attached to signing on. I felt really embarrassed and thought everyone would see me as a failure – it was such a soulless, dispiriting place to have to go. There weren't many opportunities on offer that appealed to me, and I felt stuck and hopeless, which continued for several months. Your choices are really limited when you're relying on housing benefits, so I found a cheap place to live as a lodger in a family home. The family were lovely, but my room was small and dingy, and nothing was lifting my spirits.

Then one day I saw an opportunity that awoke something in my adventurous soul – an advert asking for fit, healthy volunteers to participate in a clinical drug trial in a hospital in Leeds. I'd love to tell you that I did it to nobly advance the cause of medicine, but it may have been more to do with the £4,850 plus travel expenses on offer. Also, the opportunity to leave Hull for a while and meet some new people was massively appealing, and the whole experience changed everything for me. I met some fascinating people from all sorts of backgrounds and had some much-needed time to reflect on my life in a novel and comfortable environment. By the end of it, I found myself in a much better place and was feeling much less self-destructive. I'd made some good friends, had a laugh, earned some cash and felt much more hopeful.

For the 32 days of the trial, I was confined to the facility, which felt like a cross between a youth club and a hospital. The staff would prick you with needles several times a day to take your blood, but the food and company was great. As far as I could make out, most of the volunteers were being given the drug they were testing, while a minority of us were taking placebos. I'm pretty sure I was in the latter category, because some of the other guys were complaining about this and that, but I felt better than I had in a long time.

Most people who sign up for medical trials do it because they need the cash, so there were some students in their early twenties who were planning to use the money to fund a field trip. Other people do it to top up their earnings, and some people almost do it professionally, moving from one clinical trial to another. I remember one day, early on in the trial, we were all sat in our hospital beds, discussing what we were going to do with the money we'd earn – it was almost like we were planning for a lottery win!

One of the people I met at the clinical trial is now one of my closest friends. We share a unique relationship because we're not afraid to tell each other anything – maybe it's because we met in such an intense, weird environment and spent a lot of time bonding over competitive board games and having discussions on life, liberty and the pursuit of the perfect Sunday roast. People sometimes ask how we met, and we're always making up a new story – the last time someone asked us, we said we met at an audition for *Britain's Got Talent*!

One of the things I realised during the trial was how resilient I was. Well, it was either that or I just really hated the life I was living in Hull – and probably both. You had to be creative to pass the time, so I helped build obstacle courses on the ward to try and entertain everyone. We'd use whatever furniture we could get hold of to create giant games of snooker, or we'd make crazy golf holes, where you'd have to hit something into a container in the fewest shots you could. Some folks kept themselves to themselves, but others came out of their shells when they saw what we were up to and would join in if there was some good banter on offer. There certainly was after one of the staff put up a sign on the shower cubicle advising 'No masturbating'.

I made an effort to get on with the staff running the programme, and I made a specific effort to charm the dinner lady, who always made a banging pudding – in fact, I think that's where I developed my custard addiction. I learned how to play the board games Rummikub and Risk while I was in there, and we'd sometimes we'd have mega long games. The staff would occasionally join in, although we weren't allowed to play 'intense' board games at certain times of day because they increased our blood pressure too much – that meant Risk was off the table!

Things weren't always friendly between the staff and volunteers, and one thing we clashed over was the way in which nurses used to take our blood. They initially used a butterfly needle, which was comfortable for volunteers and if they didn't hit the vein (which would happen occasionally) they could adjust it with the needle still in, making it easy for everyone. However, then the senior management decided to stop using these needles as a cost-saving exercise and replaced them with 21-gauge needles, which relied on the nurse hitting the vein straight away. If your veins were deep or tricky to access you were screwed, because the nurse would have to pull the needle out and punch more holes in your arm until they got the vein. I shared my feelings with a bunch of the volunteers and rallied together support, quickly forming an impromptu union. Emboldened, I then went to the clinical director on behalf of all the other volunteers and managed to convince him that it was in everyone's interests to use butterfly needles. I've genuinely never been able to remain quiet when I know people are suffering needlessly. Overall, the experience invigorated me and gave me a new lease of life – I had time to mull over the direction of my life, and where I wanted to go.

With so much free time on my hands to reflect, I spent the last two weeks of the trial applying for jobs as I couldn't bear the thought of going back to my life in Hull. When the programme came to an end, some people couldn't wait to rush home and feast on their favourite junk food, but me and some of the others were really going to miss it. We'd had a truly unique experience and had learned a lot about ourselves and other people. It felt like the end of a weird yet awesome summer camp. Having trawled job sites online, I applied for several jobs and ended up getting one as a housing adviser at the homelessness charity Shelter. It wasn't what I'd hoped, though, and I left.

*   *   *

In the run-up to the UK's European Parliament election in 2014, opinion polls were charting a surge in the number of potential UKIP voters. I remember seeing the results come in on the night of 22 May 2014 and being shocked. Unlike general elections in the UK, elections to the European Parliament use proportional representation. Elections for seats in the European Parliament representing England, Scotland and Wales are distributed according to the D'Hondt system, a type of proportional representation. For the 2014 election, the UK's allocation of seats was 73; UKIP won the election with nearly 4.4 million votes, gaining 26.6 per cent of the vote and 24 Members of the European Parliament (MEPs). I was left thinking, 'Surely this can't be what we as a country voted for? Even though this is a terrible low point, we can't lose hope of a better tomorrow.' So that night, I started thinking: if I could at least try to make my small part of the world, my community in Sheffield, that little bit better, at least I would be doing something to fight the message of hate that seemed to be attracting people to UKIP.

So I started finding out what was going on in my local community, discovering who made the decisions and what I could do to influence them. One of my earliest inspirations was a guy called Mark McGowan, who is also known as the Artist Taxi Driver. No one knows if he is a genuine London taxi driver but he is definitely a performance artist and social commentator. His in-your-face approach and creative demeanour really resonated with me, and we eventually did a joint event together while I was lord mayor, titled 'Doing Politics Differently'.

I remember forcing myself to watch *Daily Politics* on the telly to find out what was happening in the world and what politics was all about. Until that point, I wondered who the hell watched these kinds of shows – they seemed so stale and boring – but now I found myself paying attention! If you'd told me then that I would appear on the last-ever *Daily Politics* show, I'd have said you were crazy.

They offered me a cup of tea in one of their famous branded mugs, which I may have 'forgotten' to return.

The first local campaign I got involved in was an effort to save Broomhill Library, after Sheffield City Council announced plans to shut it down in 2014, along with several other libraries across the city. Libraries like this are so important for providing the local community, many of whom are refugees and don't speak English as a first language, with the skills to fill out government forms, find work and improve their English. In the end we managed to save the library, which gave me a taste of what could be achieved if we energised the local community.

As for party politics, I went online and took the Vote Match test, a quiz that gives you 26 statements on policy issues that you agree or disagree with to determine the political party that best reflects your views. It came out as the Green Party, which I was pretty happy about but also surprised, as everyone I knew supported the Labour Party. The Green Party had always seemed like the good guys, honest sorts who meant well. I started looking into their policies in more detail. Number one in their 'core values' was 'supporting a radical transformation of society for the benefit of all, and for the planet as a whole'. They were also opposed to austerity and the only party who had a red line against it, as well as being in favour of free education and committed to replacing the first-past-the-post electoral system with proportional representation. In short, they seemed to care about all the issues I really cared about, especially social justice. I searched on Facebook for Natalie Bennett, who was then the leader of the party, and sent her a direct message. To my surprise, she responded almost straight away and I ended up having a proper conversation with her on Facebook, all the while being amazed at how accessible the leader of the party was. Perhaps I caught her at the right moment, but still, I marvelled at how down-to-earth and humble Natalie was to answer questions from some bloke in Sheffield. Given Natalie's friendliness and the fact that they were the only party with a red line against austerity and were in favour of scrapping tuition fees, I decided to join them.

The first Green Party event I went to was on the topic 'Is Democracy Dead?' and hosted by David Malone, an independent filmmaker, author and Green Party candidate in North Yorkshire. It was so inspiring, and the one message from it that kept going around in my head was a question he posed to the audience: 'If you're not going to get involved, who is going to make the changes you seek?' I felt like he was talking directly to me, and this moment reaffirmed my decision to join the Greens. I got more involved with the local party, met some weird and wonderful folk who really welcomed me, and campaigned in the local election in 2015. Soon after that, I stood and was elected as the fundraising officer for the local party. This built my profile and credibility within the party, so when the next local election came around, in May 2016, I'd been involved with the party for over a year. I knew I had a good chance of getting selected as the candidate for my ward, Broomhill and Sharrow Vale – I lived in the ward, campaigned in the ward and lots of people there knew me. It wasn't some strategic, ambitious decision, it just felt like a natural transition from what I'd already been doing.

That year, several local ward boundaries changed, after the Local Government Boundary Commission published the results of their electoral review. The old Central ward was divided into two, and the ward of Broomhill and Sharrow Vale was created from parts of the former Broomhill, Central and Nether Edge wards. All 84 seats in the city council were up for election – three per each of the 28 wards – so each party had to put up three candidates in each ward. Two hard-working Green councillors called Aodan Marken and Brian Webster had already been ably representing the ward, and the sole sitting Labour councillor vacated her seat and went to stand in the other side of town because she thought she'd lose – though we tried not to get too cocky, we were confident that all three seats were going to be Green.

I kept my decision to run to be a councillor quiet; I remember that my mum only found out when one of her friends saw my name and face on a campaign flyer that came through her letterbox. I was scared of disappointing people, and I've always been the sort of person that doesn't like announcing anything until I've got it. However, this approach isn't that helpful when you're trying to get elected: you need to put yourself out there.

When I'd finally convinced myself to stand, the next obstacle was being frightened of other people tearing my dream apart in its early stages. I was petrified of them laughing at me and saying, 'Don't be so stupid, Magid – what are you thinking?' Come to think of it, I think I'd always feared damning responses when I did something a little out of the ordinary. Putting yourself out there, being seen and being vulnerable are all scary things, but if there's one thing I've learned, it's that vulnerability is the birthplace of love, change and creativity.

* * *

When I was 16, I became really curious about Sheffield's Crucible Theatre and saw that they were looking for young people who'd never acted before to perform in a play about Sheffield during the summer. Never one to let a good opportunity pass me by, I signed up. I can't remember much about the play apart from the fact that I played a bus driver, though I do still have a DVD copy of it somewhere. I was really excited about being part of a team and performing in such a prestigious theatre, but there was no way on God's green earth that I could share my excitement with anyone. I grew up in a household and community where the arts weren't a viable possibility, and no one in my community did anything remotely close to theatre. So the fear of being laughed at or made to feel like I was weird made me keep it a secret. It's so stupid, reflecting back on it now. When it came to the performance, everyone else in the play had their families and friends come along, but because I hadn't told anyone, no one came. I remember when my castmates asked me where my friends were on the opening night, I panicked and said, 'They're all busy.'

My attitude to my political career is much the same: I guess I try to protect myself until I feel that something can be shared safely. So rather than tell my friends and family I was standing to be a councillor, I started my campaign by trying to drum up support among people who didn't know me. I knocked on hundreds of doors, went to every community event and made myself as visible as possible.

When the election came round, I had no idea if I'd amassed enough votes to finish in the top three. Late that night, the returning officer read out the results. 'Magid Magid: 1,882.' On one hand I was ecstatic, but I was also really upset that we hadn't done as well as a party as we'd expected. Neither of the two incumbent Green councillors, who'd both worked with me tirelessly, had received enough votes. The Labour Party had fielded two 'paper' candidates – they had done very little campaigning in the area – and both were elected alongside me. It wasn't even a target ward for them, but perhaps the result wasn't a surprise – Jeremy Corbyn was at the peak of his popularity, having been elected as Labour leader the previous September. But this didn't take away the fact that I became the first British-Somali councillor in Sheffield.

Many young people had helped get me elected. When I went knocking on doors, I found their sense of compassion really inspiring, particularly given that they were battling with the frustration that much of the electorate was unwilling to address long-term issues like air pollution. We can't just continue the way we've been living, turning our backs on 90 per cent of the world and buying ourselves out of the consequences of a warmer globe. Things can change, though – I truly believe that.

* * *

I'm greatly heartened by the work of Greta Thunberg, as well as the teenagers in Sheffield who come out every Friday to make their voices heard about the climate crisis. They're angry as hell, and terrified too. So am I, as are most of my friends in their twenties and thirties. It's truly remarkable to see so many young people galvanised and taking to the streets. When I was a young teenager I was getting up to mischief, skipping school to play with fireworks rather than campaigning to save the planet.

I was saddened to see few children from the northern suburbs of Sheffield, where I grew up, among the school strikers, but is it any wonder? It is well documented that climate change has a disproportionate impact on disadvantaged groups, yet the climate movement lacks real representation from those communities. It's vital that we take everybody with us on such an urgent cause, as the tragedy that befell Ella Kissi-Debrah shows. Ella was a nine-year-old girl who died in February 2013 from a severe asthma attack. She lived in Lewisham in south-east London, just 80 feet from the South Circular, one of the busiest roads in the capital and a pollution 'hotspot'. Her death followed three years of seizures and 27 separate hospital trips for breathing difficulties; in 2014, an inquest ruled that she died of 'acute respiratory failure' but did not investigate the role of air pollution in her death.

In 2019, Ella's mother Rosamund applied for a fresh inquest following the submission of a report by an expert which revealed that air pollution levels at a monitoring station one mile from Ella's home 'consistently' exceeded EU pollution limits during the three years before her death. It was also revealed that the asthma attack that resulted in Ella's death coincided with one of the worst air pollution surges in the area, concluding that there was a 'real prospect that without unlawful levels of air pollution, Ella would not have died'.

Thanks to Rosamund's tenacity, the 2014 inquest was quashed and a fresh one has been scheduled for later in 2020. It is quite possible that Ella may be the first person whose cause of death is listed as air pollution. This is a tragic example of how poor communities, which frequently are also ethnic minorities, and often concentrated around main roads in major cities, suffer the consequences of decisions made by people who often have no idea of their plight. They have the dirtiest industries in their backyards; their children have asthma and there are frequent cancer clusters. These communities suffer the consequences of decisions made by the wealthy elites and their cutthroat corporations. Lewisham is one such place and remains among the most deprived local authority areas in England, according to the Index of Multiple Deprivation

(2015). You cannot have climate justice without social justice. Rosamund has fought tirelessly for what's right, never losing hope and holding onto the belief that despite experiencing such a personal tragedy, people in similar positions as Ella shouldn't suffer the same fate. Rosamund's tenacity illustrates the importance of hanging on to hope – even in the most challenging of circumstances.

The front lines of this fight are in the marginalised edges of global power, with the poor, the more vulnerable and those beyond the easy embrace of development. They will pay the catastrophic consequences of a world spinning its way into oblivion. I salute those who are shaking us. I salute the climate strikers skipping school to save school, the local community activists fighting for justice, the extinction rebels disrupting indifference and the countless young activists like Isra Hirsi and Xiye Bastida who are proving no-one is ever too small to make a difference. Most importantly of all, I salute the countless unnamed activists who are fighting in the face of the consequences of corporate greed. We must be diverse in our voices, strategies and actions. And we must act now.

* * *

I know it might sound corny, but in the face of our present crises, the only real solution is hope. Hope is, I think, a type of kindness – to ourselves, to one another and to the rest of the world – that makes getting through the dark times possible. There will be dark times ahead, but hope is what opens up the future beyond that, providing the fuel that drives us to keep going. Hope is what keeps us committed to a life well-lived, in connection with others, even when those connections are hard to come by and we feel overwhelmed by everything in the world that sucks. Hope is what makes fighting against injustices bearable. It is what makes our fight against extinction smart and disciplined rather than random and self-destructive. And we *will* need to fight.

Hope is what the far right has given up on when their leaders choose to peddle fear, closing hearts and doors. And right now we need clear minds and open arms. Hope is what keeps us open to the world and to others, and so much is trying to close that down, keeping us in a rat race we never chose to participate in it, as Brad Pitt says in *Fight Club*, we are 'chasing cars and clothes, working jobs we hate, so we can buy shit we don't need.' But we have our great challenge, our heroic collective task: we have ten short years (according to the latest report from the UN Intergovernmental Panel on Climate Change) to give ourselves a fighting chance to avert the worst effects of climate catastrophe. We also have the urgent responsibility to stand up for people from under-represented communities – people of colour, the LGBT+ community and those from disadvantaged backgrounds who are likely to suffer the most.

In the face of grave threats, it is easy to despair. Who has not felt the weight of disappointment or disillusionment once or twice in their lives? But we must hope, because it works. I'm not talking about a naive kind of hope, the belief that all our problems can just disappear but a wise and challenging one where we recognise that the path ahead will be difficult but worth the effort.

We must choose hope because action is better than inaction. We must choose hope because compassion is better than hate. We must choose hope because community and belonging are better than isolation and fear. And ultimately, we must choose hope because the alternative is too bleak to sit this one out and wait for the next chance as there just might not be another one.

We can sometimes talk about hope so much you can forgive one for being highly suspicious of it – it can be too abstract. I get it. Just having hope can be too detached and too passive. Hope is not a strategy, and without a plan, it's just a wish. Alongside having hope, we have to set goals and work out how we achieve these goals through action. We have to be participants, agents and a force for good: as well as having hope, we must be a hope, too.

Hope is difficult because it is an emotional risk – I get it. Couple hope with action. Rather than being led by governments, policymakers or political leaders, why not join a union, volunteer, start a petition or join a campaign? There's always some action you can take, and even in the most difficult of circumstances, there is always hope. Because let's face it, if it wasn't for love, hope and compassion, my story would not have come to pass. And if you look at your own life, you'll find glimpses of light amid the darkness that are evidence of another, better world. Hope transcends our existence – in work, our personal lives and politics. It is the undying belief that a better world is not only theoretically possible but achievable, and within reach. That's why we need to foster hope in ourselves and in others – so that we might move away from a world motivated by profit, competition and hate, and towards one motivated by cooperation, kindness and love.

VI
DO IT DIFFERENTLY

*'Plants are more courageous than almost all human beings:
an orange tree would rather die than produce lemons, whereas
instead of dying the average person would rather be
someone they are not.'*

Mokokoma Mokhonoana

At university, I was that person who's involved in pretty much everything. You'd see me everywhere. At house parties I was the overly energetic one, dancing like I was high while I was actually completely sober. On campus, I was the one handing you a flyer for a student event. At the university sports centre, I was instructing the mixed martial arts (MMA) team that I'd founded. These extra-curricular experiences while I was a student helped shape who I am today, but it was being part of the MMA club that gave me my first political awakening. Whatever position I've found myself in, I've attempted to use my platform to draw awareness to important causes which don't get the attention they deserve, and to bring people together.

Initially, I just wanted the students' union to help fund the MMA club, so we could have better equipment and not have to share mats with the cheerleading club (as charming as they were). But after meeting other sports club presidents, I quickly realised that other sports clubs had similar issues. Knowing the value sports teams held for students, this became the first campaign I was involved in. I soon realised that there were lots of other issues at university that I wanted to do something about, such as eradicating

135

hidden course costs that leave many students out of pocket when they need to buy expensive textbooks, undertaking research trips or course equipment. Putting these kinds of things right appealed to my inquisitive nature, my love of challenges and my courage to stand up for what I believed in, so I decided to stand for students' union president. At that time I couldn't have told you the difference between left and right in politics, but I knew the issues I cared about. I didn't know how to go about campaigning and I had no idea what had been done before – all I knew was that me and my friends had problems, and the students' union wasn't helping us as much as we needed it to.

When I started to run my campaign, I soon found out that the vast majority of previous presidents of Hull University Union had been politics students and members of political societies. I began to feel like an imposter and had serious self-doubt regarding my capability and chances of success. But I figured I'd give it a go, and threw everything I had into putting together a fun and engaging campaign. This set me apart from the other candidates, most of whom were studying politics and ran very conventional campaigns. I did things differently: I was honest, upfront and relatable, and I wasn't trying to be someone I wasn't. But above all, I listened and shared my feelings. I engaged with people. No matter what the media or an episode of *House of Cards* tell you, this is the real core of politics. To those people who are already in politics or activism, if you don't engage with people, then – I hate to echo what some of your intimate partners may have said – but you're doing it wrong! I failed to get re-elected as students' union president, through a combination of not being as organised as I should have been and smear attacks from my opponent which I didn't know how to deal with. I learnt a lot from these mistakes.

I'm not saying do everything differently – there are some things you definitely shouldn't do differently, like CPR. What I am saying is that if you can truly discover your authenticity – what makes you stand out – you can unlock a lot of power. If you throw a bit of creativity into the mix, there's no limit to what you can achieve. Henry Ford once said, 'If you always do what you've always done, you'll always get what you've always got,' and I think there's a lot of truth in that. If you really want to engage and connect with people in any line of work, stepping out of your comfort zone or going off the beaten track is the way to go. People stick to what they know because it's safe, but a lot of power comes from refusing to conform.

Sometimes I'll have no idea what's going to happen, but I know that doing something the way it's always been done either has not been working or has not brought about the change that I seek. So I figure, what have I got to lose?

If you're looking to set up any business or launch any kind of campaign, you need to find your USP that sets you apart. I'm constantly thinking, 'How can I get an edge?' A lot of athletes look for ways to gain an advantage over their rivals, whether it's going vegan or trying cupping therapy. Former American competitive swimmer Michael Phelps used to sleep in an altitude chamber so his body would produce more red blood cells. Everyone is trying to be more effective and get better results, whether in sport or work. You needn't fork out for an underwater treadmill, but do try to find a way to give you something that others don't have.

If I'm lucky, an idea will come to me quickly, but sometimes I have to sit down and go through a hundred things until inspiration strikes. Then I'll sometimes just run with the idea or, if doubts start to creep in, I'll ask two close friends for their advice. I've got a friend who I'll affectionately call the most 'traditional' person I know, who will often pose questions that I wouldn't have considered. A conversation with him also helps me to develop a counter-argument, so I can work out how to defend my position if I need to. He's getting increasingly mad that I'm not listening to his advice, but I am — it's really useful, but I'm just not following it. Sometimes I feel like I know exactly what he's going to say because it's stuff that I've already thought of, but I can also be pleasantly surprised by his encouragement — it's only when he's 100 per cent supportive of one of my ideas that I start to worry! There's always something useful to take from his advice.

People often accuse me of tearing up tradition, but what *is* tradition, apart from peer pressure from dead people? When I started the MMA club at university, I was able to create traditions from the outset, which was really exciting, and I could also adapt existing ones to reflect what we were about. I decided to keep the idea of wearing club ties but I wanted to jazz them up a bit, so we went for my then-favourite colour, a kind of royal purple. I also devised the club's motto — 'Pursuit, Pain and Passion'. Like other clubs, we had initiation ceremonies for new recruits, but we did things in a more community-minded way. All new recruits had to cross the Humber Bridge — a distance of 1.38 miles — only they had to do it on all fours, and each of them would get their friends and family to sponsor them and raise money for a local charity. All the other sports societies at the university were sponsored by takeaway or other local businesses, but I thought it would be great if we sponsored a charity instead. So we sponsored KIDS, a charity that provides support to disabled children, young people and their families. We were doing a good deed but also raising the profile of the charity, so it felt like a win-win. These small changes meant that we stood out as a club that was doing things differently. I still go back every year for the club's annual presentation evening – they created 'The Magic Magid Award for Outstanding Contribution', which is such an honour, and so I present it each year and give a speech. It will be the tenth anniversary this year, so we'll bring back a lot of old boys and girls for a big do. And if I find that the students running the club have decided to change any of the traditions I started, then I'll understand!

One thing I established in Sheffield that I'm immensely proud of is the post of Sheffield's poet laureate. Nobody suggested I should do it or gave me permission to do it, but with the backing of many local creatives and allies like Professor Vanessa

Toulmin, Director of City and Culture at the University of Sheffield, we launched the idea at the Off the Shelf literary festival in 2018. I wanted someone to champion the creative arts in Sheffield in new and exciting ways. And who did I appoint? Step up Otis Mensah. A 23-year-old, self-described working-class radical hip-hop artist, poet and storyteller. He has supported the likes of the Wu-Tang Clan and the Sugarhill Gang, performed his experimental hip hop set on the BBC Introducing stage at Glastonbury and has recently released his second collection of poetry. For me, Otis represents everything that is great about Sheffield – he's dynamic, skilful and radical. While the response to his appointment was overwhelmingly positive, some comments made it clear that poetry is still massively affected by elitism while others were just plain racist. Yes, Otis is the first hip hop artist to be awarded such a title in the UK, and I'm proud that he's breaking down barriers, smashing stuffy stereotypes and reminding people that poetry is meant to be for the people. Otis also reminds us all of the power of being bold, brave – of daring to be different.

*   *   *

When I got elected as a councillor, for the Green Party I felt a responsibility to support and give a platform to other people who shared my 'Do Things Differently' approach – I hoped that some of them would go on to make fantastic councillors themselves. In 2016 I met Kaltum Rivers, an amazing mother-of-four and a community activist who had lived in Broomhall since 2005. Like me, she was a refugee from Somalia. She'd also been a parent governor at Broomhall Nursery and a local infant school. I saw the potential in Kaltum, so I encouraged her to get involved and supported her along the way. She ended up being elected in the Sheffield City Council election in 2018 with nearly 50 per cent of the vote, taking the seat from Labour. It was one of the proudest moments of my life and it has been heart-warming to see her go from strength to strength.

In 2019, my council seat was up for election. I'd always said from the moment I decided to stand as a councillor that I would do one term and then move on to something else – I've never really enjoyed doing something for a long period and wanted to stay true to my philosophy of taking myself out of my comfort zone. So I was looking for a successor to take my seat as councillor for Broomhill and

Sharrow Vale and thought I'd found the perfect person in Angela Argenzio, who had moved to Sheffield from Italy 23 years ago earlier and become a secondary school teacher. She wasn't a member of a political party, but she was a trustee at City of Sanctuary, a finance manager for Sheffield Royal Society for the Blind and part of Hope not Hate, the advocacy group that campaigns against racism and fascism. She was compassionate, committed and approachable, all attributes that you need to be a councillor – I just knew that she would make an amazing representative. I also felt that at a time when Brexit dominated everything, it was important to have an EU citizen as a councillor to give a voice to all the EU citizens in the city.

I sent Angela a message on Facebook to ask her if she'd consider joining the Green Party and standing for election in Broomhill and Sharrow Vale. The deadline was looming and she'd need to start immediately, but having talked to her family, she put herself up and got selected as the candidate. And when the election came round, she won with 58.5 per cent of the vote. I was so proud of her and would be lying if I said I didn't have a tear in my eye. She's now one of the best councillors Sheffield has.

It was at an unprecedented time for the Green Party in Sheffield – the fact that we had four councillors meant that we could nominate a candidate for lord mayor. However, the process was a little more long-winded than that because the lord mayor is usually the person who has served as deputy mayor the previous year – it's almost a formality. So I put myself forward for the position of deputy lord mayor with the support of my fellow Green councillors, which was approved by a motion of the other council members. However, there was no guarantee that I would become lord mayor the following year, especially given the game of political football that was being played in the council chamber, as events on 5 April 2017 were to show.

At a full council meeting, the Green councillor Alison Teal, a great inspiration of mine and a great example of what an elected politician should be, accused the Labour councillor Bryan Lodge of 'misleading' the public about the city council's hugely controversial tree-felling programme and provided evidence to support her allegation. The Labour group, who had a 'we know best' approach and at times acted like a dictatorship thanks to their number of councillors, asked her to withdraw the claim. Alison, being the courageous person she is, refused, so the Labour group decided to pass a motion to remove her from the chamber, which they won 49 votes to 21.

Alison left the chamber, but my fellow Green councillors and I followed her in protest, as did all the other opposition councillors. This was portrayed as a disrespectful act towards the sitting lord mayor who was chairing the meeting, but the reality was that we wanted to show solidarity with Alison and convey that the truth will not be silenced – it had nothing to do with the lord mayor. After this had happened, senior members of the Labour group made it clear to me that I would not have their support if I was thinking of standing for lord mayor. Since they held 53 of the 84 seats, and I'd need a majority, it looked like a tall order.

Nevertheless, I put myself forward. I knew I had the support of all the Liberal Democrat opposition councillors, as well as a number of Labour councillors. Some of them would regularly inform me of what was going on within the Labour group and if my name came up, which it frequently seemed to. Then one day I was invited to the local football derby, Sheffield United against Sheffield Wednesday, along with the Labour leader of the council, Julie Dore. She was an Owl and I was a Blade, and some bright spark thought it was a good idea to sit us together. At halftime, after a few drinks, she ended up being quite open with me and sharing all sorts of things. I was shocked when she told me that the number-one topic the Labour councillors spent most time talking about in their meetings was not how they were going to tackle homelessness and not what the council should do to support young people or mental health – it was me. I was both baffled and concerned as the Labour group were supposed to be running the city.

On another occasion, Julie told me that if I wanted them to vote for me to become lord mayor, I would need to write a public letter of apology to the Labour Party for taking part in the much-publicised walkout. Thankfully, I'm not as stupid as she probably hoped I would be – I knew they just wanted some ammunition to attack the Green Party with. There was so much of this kind of petty political bullshit – it was ridiculous. Although the community I represented and myself initially believed that our voices mattered and that the council would listen, the Labour group reminded us that was not the case. The council functioned a bit like an autocracy – all the decisions are made by the leader of the council, who chooses a nine-person cabinet and essentially tells his or her councillors how to vote. It's referred to as the 'strong leader model', and it means that only 10 out of the 84 councillors have the power to make the decisions that impact the half-million residents of Sheffield.

Thankfully, it looks like things are beginning to change. During my tenure as lord mayor, I learned about a fantastic campaign called 'It's Our City', which sets out to do things differently. They wanted to change the strong leader model to something known as the modern committee system, a more inclusive and collaborative system in which each councillor has much more impact over the council's decision-making. It's Our City started a petition, which I was happy to launch as lord mayor, but in order to trigger a referendum to change the council system, it needed to be signed by 5 per cent of the voters in the city – 20,092 people. However, such is the appetite for change that last year they collected over 26,000 signatures and a referendum has been triggered. The petition also had other effects: just hours after it had been submitted, the council's deputy leader Olivia Blake resigned and pledged to support It's Our City, although that may have had more to do with her upcoming bid to stand as an MP the need to distance herself from the council. Soon after she resigned, one cabinet member and three more councillors came out against the Labour council leadership. If the It's Our City campaign succeeds, it could represent a trailblazing example of how to bring about change in a city.

This mission of this council should be to turn love into policies and to make the whole world fall in love with Sheffield. I know it's a massive ambition to have – making the whole world fall in love with just one city. But I know it's possible.

To all the councillors and those in leadership roles, for our city to flourish, I say this: have the biggest ambitions, let your imagination be the limits of what's possible. The shopkeeper of forty-three years, the struggling artist, the single mother, the newly arrived refugee, the far from home student, the hundreds of thousands of people with intertwined dreams living between these seven hills and five rivers are begging you to see no limits and fear no critics.

I was eventually surprised to learn that the Labour group were not going to put up a candidate to oppose me in my mayoral campaign, and it was only in early May 2018 that I finally believed that I was going to be lord mayor of my beloved home city. At that point I decided to tell my mum. I went round to her house for a cup of tea and to pick up my post and asked her to leave the date of 16 May free, because there was a chance I might become lord mayor. I think she said, 'What do you mean you're going to be lord mayor?' but it sounded so ridiculous that she repeated the question a couple more times.

After that initial disbelief, she got excited and started ringing every family member she could to tell them the news. I told her that among the other important council duties I would be responsible for, I would get a gold chain, a really cool office and a chauffeur. She was so proud of me, prayed for me and wished me well. If I'd followed her advice, I would have become an engineer, a doctor or a lawyer. I would have been the most devoutly religious Muslim you could imagine, married at 24 with a couple of kids, but I just wasn't that guy. She could never have predicted what I've ended up doing, but I think she understands what drives me now. She knows I want to work hard and do things my own way, but also, most importantly, that I want to make a positive contribution to society.

On 16 May 2018, Councillor Alison Teal moved a motion to appoint me the 122nd Lord Mayor of

Sheffield, stating: 'There is nothing faint-hearted about Magid. I am confident that he will prove time and again as our first citizen that despite his youth compared to most of us in this chamber, he has the wit and self-assurance to make a tremendous success of this latest adventure that he is embarking upon. I, along with my Green colleagues in particular, would like to wish Magid every success in his role of mayor, and I heartily recommend him to the chamber.'

Alison's motion was seconded, as the constitution demands, by Councillor Bob Pullin, who said, 'I would very much like, on the basis of Magid Magid's social commitment, character and his positive outlook for positive change, to say that I am pleased to commend him to you all as a fit and proper person to be lord mayor and first citizen, with every confidence for the City of Sheffield.'

I then took my oath in front of a full council chamber, pretty certain that some people there couldn't quite believe what was happening:

'I, Councillor Magid Magid, have been appointed to the office of Lord Mayor of the City of Sheffield. I hereby declare that I take that office upon myself and I will duly

and faithfully fulfil the duties in the accord-
ance of the best of my judgment and ability. I undertake to observe the code as to
conduct that is expected of members of the
Sheffield City Council.'

As a Muslim, one of my favourite times of the year is
Ramadhan, the holy ninth month in the Islamic cal-
endar, but one annoying thing is that it's not at the
same time each year – the starting date is determined
by the arrival of the new moon. Even as the first citizen of Sheffield, I don't get a seat on the Ramadhan
moon sighting committee, so I didn't know if the
day I was to take my oath as lord mayor was going
to coincide with the first day of Ramadhan. It's usually traditional for the lord mayor to welcome guests
at the inauguration with a fancy spread of food, but
I didn't plan that because I wasn't sure whether I
would be fasting. In short, if I was fasting, everyone
else was going to be – there was no way they were
going to have food and drink at my party when I
couldn't! In the end, Ramadhan began the day after
my inauguration, which meant the councillors and I
could celebrate with a drink, along with assembled
friends and family.

I invited the amazing and loyal collection of people who I now regard as my best friends – they have grounded me, supported me and shaped me into the person I am today. There were also two very important guests: my Year 3 teacher, Miss Simpson (or 'Cheryl' as she now keeps asking me to call her, which still feels odd!). I mentioned her in my speech, praising her patience and unwavering belief that I would make something of myself. The other VIP was my mum. Her countless sacrifices had made my achievements possible, so I asked her to stand up while I said a few words about her. I didn't expect the entire council chamber to rise to their feet in applause but they did, which touched her deeply.

I also shared a story about an experience I'd had while appearing on the TV series *Hunted* the previous year to make a point about how welcoming the people of Sheffield are. On the programme, contestants or 'fugitives' try to evade experts who attempt to hunt them down within 25 days. We'd started in Manchester city centre and there was a point while I was on the run where I found myself in the middle of nowhere, somewhere in North Yorkshire. I was hungry, thirsty, tired and probably smelly too – surrounded by nothing but fields, country roads and

Conservative election posters, and with the sun beating down on me, I was at a low point. After hours and hours of trying to hitch a ride with no luck, I was in despair, when a Skoda Yeti pulled up. 'Are you alright? Can I help you?' the driver said. Not only did he stop and give me a ride – he also welcomed me into his home and introduced me to his family. They gave me a bed and even baked me a Victoria sponge. Despite the climate of fear we live in, that man and his family showed me nothing but love, hospitality and warmth, and I will never forget it. Now it just so happens that the gentleman – Tony Russell-Ward – lives in Crookes, a suburb of Sheffield. I think Tony and his family embody everything that is great about our city.

The message of my speech was simple – I wasn't here to change the world, but if I could play any part in changing our lives for the better, I would consider my role as lord mayor fulfilled. And I vowed to work tirelessly, visiting schools, communities, businesses and charities to share stories, thank volunteers and tell young people that they could achieve anything. I ended my speech by saying that the very act of me obtaining such a position was a celebration of Sheffield rather than of me, and were it not for the people's love, compassion and courage, my not this story would have not been told. That's why, when I became lord mayor, this was the first message I put out:

> Me and my family moved to Sheffield from Somalia when I was five years old to look for a better life, and it was this great city I call home that welcomed me and many others like me.
>
> Fast forward to today, and I am honoured and privileged to have been given the highest honour that can be bestowed upon any citizen in this city.
>
> But I am not arrogant enough to think that I made it here all by myself. I want and need you all to know that today is as much a celebration about YOU as it is about me.
>
> Regardless of how minor or major, you have played a role in shaping me into the person I am today. Whether we met in Sheffield, Hull, worked together, met in a random place or had a fleeting encounter, I am eternally grateful.
>
> Thank you and God bless.

His right worshipful, the first citizen of Sheffield, the Lord Mayor of Sheffield, Cllr Magid (or just Magid to you) x

On my first day as lord mayor, there was a moment when I was in the lord mayor's parlour by myself for around 30 minutes, just pacing up and down as I tried to absorb it all. I remember thinking to myself, 'I can't imagine that the people who built this parlour would have ever thought that a black, Muslim refugee would have ever been lord mayor.' It was a time of reflection – I was both thankful and grateful, but I was also thinking, 'What am I going to do; how am I going to make the most of this remarkable opportunity?'

A few days before, instead of using the same photographer the council uses for mayoral portraits, I'd hired my own photographer, Chris Saunders, to take the photograph. This would then hang in the ante-room, along with the photographs of the previous 121 lord mayors. As I looked up at all the portraits, the photographs didn't say anything to me, other than that the previous lord mayors all did the job in much the same way. I thought it would have been amazing if they'd chosen to do something more creative with their portraits, so each one said something unique about them, what they dreamed about or hoped to achieve. I wanted mine to say, 'I'm here to do things differently, but at the same time I'm here to have as much of an impact as possible.'

I appreciated that this picture was going to outlast me, so what I chose to wear for it was important. I went for a three-piece suit, the gold Casio calculator watch that I'd been wearing for the previous six years and some Dr Martens boots. It was one of the rare occasions that I did dress up, but I did it for me and to look sharp, rather than to obey any convention. I get a lot of questions about my choice of clothes, but I've been the same for as long as I can remember – it's just my environment that keeps changing. Even when I was a councillor, I'd generally wear a hoodie and T-shirt or some other informal get-up. I've never felt the need to impress people by changing into something more formal. Don't get me wrong, if you invite me to your wedding, you had best believe I'll be super smart, but I'll do it my own way. I've always tried to be true to myself in what I choose to wear, and I see how people respond to that authenticity. People often ask how I can have the courage to be myself in an environment that tells me

I shouldn't be, but I think it just comes from my 'I want to be free to be me' attitude and the value I've learned in being unapologetically myself. The people who don't like me are never going to like me, but maybe some of will respect me because I don't try to be someone I'm not. I'm never going to please everyone: if you try to be everyone's cup of tea, you might as well be a mug.

Walking through the town hall, Chris and I took lots of generic photos, because I didn't know exactly what I was after for my portrait. Being the genius he is, he thought it would make a great shot if I stood on the plinth on one side of the main staircase, which had a sizeable drop on the other side. Before I got on it, I had to make sure that there were no security officers around – they would definitely have told me to get down, and rightly so! After taking a couple of shots of me standing up, I decided to squat to gain balance, and when we were reviewing the pictures, I just knew that was the one. I posted the shot on Twitter on the day of my inauguration, along with the message, 'Holy shit, this is surreal! With love, courage and opportunity literally anything is possible!' Things went crazy after that, when the tweet went viral. People like Skepta, Rageh Omaar and

George Takei, who I had always admired, were sharing my picture and story.

It was only when Ramadhan was over, 30 days later, that I had a proper inauguration do, with a sit-down meal and a party – because what's a party without food or drink? It actually felt a bit like a wedding. Everyone that I would have wanted at my wedding was there, including all my family and friends, some of whom had come from Scarborough, Spain and Somalia. It was a special occasion because it was the first time that all my siblings and nephews and nieces had come together in one place. The ceremony was at lunchtime, followed by official photographs food.

I remember giving myself a pep talk before my speech, telling myself that I'd been given an amazing opportunity but that I needed to step up to the plate and really own it. I knew it was going to be difficult and that I was going to make mistakes, but I had one shot and I had to make it count. I shouldn't care about what the naysayers were telling me, because in a year's time, I figured that no one would be worrying about it. I made a big deal about my mum in the speech. I wrote it on the day, but I knew what I'd say some time before that – it was all in my head. I mentioned tradition and praised Sheffield. The macebearer, Julie, who'd worked with 32 lord mayors before me, said: 'That was the best speech I've heard from a lord mayor,' but maybe she says that to everyone! It set the tone for my friendship with Julie – she was my right-hand woman and always had my back because she understood that my heart was in the right place.

After that, I threw a party at the Picture House Social in Nether Edge, south of the city centre, that was opened up to the public. There were so many people there and I think I posed for selfies for two hours straight. It was an amazing night – people felt part of the celebrations, which was the whole point.

*   *   *

I think I ended up as lord mayor because there was a feeling that it might be good for the city and people wanted change. The Labour group were split on whether it was a smart move, but I think a lot of that was just party politics. I'm sure that if I'd been a Labour councillor – and several of the Labour group had encouraged me to defect to them from the Greens on numerous occasions – they would have fully supported me. However, some of the Labour councillors told me early in my tenure that they regretted voting for me – they thought I'd disrespected the city by not following its traditions like toasting the Queen (I chose to toast the City of Sheffield instead). I don't hate the Queen – I think she works really hard – but I think the monarchy is an outdated system and should be replaced with an elected head of state. Some Labour councillors were supportive, praising me for making the role my own, for engaging with so many people and for putting Sheffield on the map.

I think some people, and especially my fellow councillors, assumed that I'd conform when I became lord mayor. The tradition was to be impartial during your year of office and not get involved in any contentious political issues, but this had often been flouted by previous lord mayors – after all, everything you do as mayor is political in some way, even choosing to remain silent. I wanted to use my platform to campaign for the changes I wanted to see and to be a voice for those who felt they didn't have one.

It was also traditional for lord mayors to remain neutral on the subject of football and not admit to favouring either one of the two Sheffield football clubs, Wednesday or United. The idea was that you were supposed to represent the whole city and therefore both clubs, but any football fan will tell you that's not possible! As I've mentioned, I'm a proud United fan, and that goes all the way back to my childhood. The club is really community-minded and puts on games at their academy for underprivileged kids. I fondly remember playing at a few of their events and also recall reading about Arthur Wharton, the first black professional footballer, playing for Sheffield United, which speaks volumes about the city's diverse history.

I remained neutral when it was important to do so, like when I was chairing council meetings – oddly, this actually represented a return to tradition! In previous years, even though Labour had had a large majority in the council chamber for some time, Labour lord mayors had voted for and against motions, rather than remaining neutral. I always found this bizarre, because Labour had the votes anyway – they didn't need the lord mayor's vote. Showing bias when you're supposed to be chairing a meeting is wrong and does a disservice to the public. Of course, there were numerous times when I would make decisions that the Labour cabinet were against, but when it came to chairing the council meetings, I was very careful to treat everyone equally. I would cut the speakers off after they'd used their allotted time. Some of the Labour councillors would routinely exceed their permitted time and previous Labour lord mayors had turned a blind eye but I didn't let them, so no one could accuse me of bias. I treated my fellow Green councillors the same way, too. As much as the Labour group hated it, it forced them to be more concise and better prepared, encouraging efficiency. I think they appreciated that in the end, and the civil servants were certainly grateful!

Though it is not well known, council meetings are open to everyone and members of the public can attend and sit in the public gallery to observe or ask questions to the cabinet. Members of the public would often get really passionate over various political causes and at times even stage a peaceful protest, which would include bringing in their own banners. Whereas the previous lord mayors would get security to remove them, I would control the situation and allow them to peacefully protest, as was their right. I used the half-hour interval in the monthly council meeting I chaired to showcase Sheffield's creative talent, inviting poets, comedians and artists to perform. I wanted ordinary citizens to feel like they owned the chamber, and Sheffield's councillors to see the value in the creative talent that this great city had to offer.

I'm sad to say that a number of councillors objected to the idea, and up to half of them would stand outside the chamber in protest during the performances, returning to the chamber once they had finished. This felt petty and pathetic to me. It wasn't me they were offending, it was the young creative people who'd been looking forward to the opportunity. Some of the councillors would complain to the chief executive of the council and expect him to do something, but he'd tell them that I was the lord mayor and could do what I liked in the meetings I chaired. That annoyed them so much!

Occasionally, members of the public would submit 'emergency questions' on the day of a council meeting. It was up to me whether I accepted or rejected them, and against the advice of the chief executive of the council I accepted some of them. Councillors hated being held to account by questions they were unable to prepare for because they feared being exposed. When people have been used to having all the power and someone comes along who does something differently without following the established customs and traditions, they don't know how to react.

Every month I would run a campaign to highlight a particular issue and share it on my social media platforms. It would always involve me squatting somewhere in the Town Hall and wearing a pair of Dr Martens boots, a hat and a T-shirt with a political message. I would share the picture on the same day as the full council meeting, right before going in to chair the meeting, dressed exactly as I was in the picture. In January 2019, I did one that celebrated the NHS and criticised the government. For the photograph, I squatted on a desk with a coffin behind me (a prop I'd borrowed from the Crucible Theatre). I held a meeting in my office with the whips of each political party a day before the full council meeting, as usual, and one of them asked about the coffin – rightly so, as not many people have coffins lying around their office! Jokingly, I said that I was going to do a bit of performance theatre at tomorrow's full council meeting: I would be brought in inside the coffin, which would be placed on the table in front of the lord mayor's seat, before rising from it.

I later found out from a source that the Labour group spent most of a two-hour meeting discussing what they would do if I pulled that stunt. They were bizarrely fixated on me, which wasted so much valuable time, but also showed me how easily I could wind them up.

When I talk to friends and Labour activists in other parts of the country about local politics, many tell me that they use Sheffield Council as an example of how not to run a council. The council is notorious for protecting the interests of private finance initiatives (PFIs), that outsource jobs formerly managed by the council to private companies, above its own citizens.

For example, take the hugely controversial Streets Ahead highways maintenance contract with Amey plc, which has led to the felling of thousands of healthy trees around Sheffield and will cost taxpayers £2.2 billion over 25 years. The contract was finalised under a Labour-led council and signed in 2012, but it was not publicly available and if you dared to ask for any details, you would have been told you couldn't have that information due to 'commercial confidentiality'. If you are dealing with public money, contracts should never be handled in private. It was only after repeated freedom of information requests that the council have released some of the documents, albeit with some details redacted.

In July 2019, the Forestry Commission concluded their 15-month investigation into whether the felling of 5,400 of Sheffield's street trees had been carried out illegally. They strongly criticised the council for 'falling far short of good practice', accusing them of failing to provide information to investigators and engage with local residents, and also of not keeping records of the trees they felled.

After the council finally released the redacted documents, it was revealed that healthy trees had been felled because their contract with Amey required a 'straight kerb line', even though the Highways Act doesn't require this. The council had previously claimed that felling healthy trees was only ever a 'last resort' but the Forestry Commission rubbished this notion, pointing to several other options the council could have taken. Also, despite claiming that Amey had never been given a 'target' number of trees to fell and replace, the freedom of information request revealed that the council had inserted the requirement that Amey replace the trees 'at a rate of not less than 200 per year so that 17,500 highway trees are replaced' by the end of the contract, with the penalty of pay deductions if they didn't meet the target. As a result of being publicly shamed, the council acknowledged that 'a change of approach was crucial for moving forwards' in December 2019 and agreed an action plan with Amey and Sheffield Trees Action Groups (STAG) to manage the city's trees. Having the courage to call people and organizations out, forces them to change: and doing things differently pays off.

One of the things I learned early on in my tenure as lord mayor was that citizens wanted to know who was representing them and who they could go to when they needed help. Some people seemed to think I was some 'Supreme Ruler of Sheffield' and had all the power in the world, but I didn't – I was just much more visible and approachable than other leaders in Sheffield. My encounters with members of the public were almost entirely positive and often heart-warming – it was inside the town hall that I found myself encountering resistance at every turn.

One particular person I had to work with closely was very difficult. Three previous lord mayors had also experienced real difficulties working with her, but despite many complaints being made about her to the chief executive, nothing happened. She would frequently make racist, sweeping comments, like 'All Jamaicans are lazy,' but when I complained about to her superior and suggested she should take some sort of cultural diversity training, it was ignored.

THE ART OF DISRUPTION

I'll never forget the first time this person freaked out and told me, 'Who do you think you are? You're ruining everything,' after I'd said I wasn't going to wear a gown for the official portrait, refused to appoint the lord mayor's chaplain (who was meant to spiritually guide me in my year of office) and declined to appoint a consort to accompany me to official functions and events. The formal tradition is that if you're married to a woman, her official title would be 'lady mayoress' and if you're a female lord mayor, your husband's official title would be 'lord mayor's consort'. And if you're unmarried, like I was, but had a girlfriend, her official title would be 'lord mayor's escort'. Seriously! Irrespective of the 'title', I felt that having the same person accompany me to all my engagements could become boring, so I decided that I would invite ordinary citizens to be my plus ones, mainly through social media shout-outs. My chauffeur Carl and I would pick them up, they'd accompany me to the event and we'd drop them off at home later. It felt like a good way to share as much of the experience of being lord mayor with as many different people as possible.

It's funny how people can get so emotional about protecting the status quo. When people say 'We've always done it like this' to justify their actions, I think about appalling traditions like slavery or women not having the vote. Some things have to change, especially when they're cruel, unfair or unfit for purpose – we're not in the 1950s anymore. Sometimes you have to shake things up to bring about change, like when Rosa Parks refused to move from her seat on the bus or when Anne Kent and Anne Knight founded the first women's suffrage movement in the UK – the Sheffield Female Political Association – in 1851.

I'd often find myself putting on public events with hardly any support from the council. These were events that should have united the city, like a mental health fundraising event I organised with Jon McClure, lead singer of the band Reverend and The Makers and a vocal supporter of mine, or an event called 'Love Sheffield Day' that I planned to coincide with the end of my tenure as lord mayor. There had been individual events focused on specific things before, but not something like this that brought the city together. There was lots of local literary, musical and cultural talent, along with a funfair, kids entertainment and food. You'd have thought everyone at the council would have been behind this celebration of the city, but they weren't.

Usually the lord mayor is able to use the council's communications team to help with press enquiries and general communications, so it was quite telling when someone from the communications team told me that he and his team had been instructed not to get involved with anything I was doing. Maybe the council thought I was unruly and too much of a liability so didn't want to get involved, despite me saying regularly that we should work together. Another theory is that the Labour group didn't want my profile to grow any bigger because they felt threatened by my increased influence. I think both theories were correct. Anyway, the lack of council support made life difficult for me, especially with all the media and interview requests I was receiving by this time. Having to navigate those by myself and sometimes falling into journalists' traps made me learn quickly.

It got to a point, in the middle of my term, when the Labour councillors could no longer tolerate me. Following a petition to remove me from my role because I supposedly 'brought the office into disrepute' (which got 2126 signatures compared to the counter petition to keep me in my role that got 19,018 signatures), some of them introduced a motion that would change the constitution and limit the roles and responsibilities of the lord mayor. This had never happened before. They were basically trying to stop me from being me, but they made a real cock-up of it: they brought the motion to a full council meeting, but realised midway through that not only did they not have the numbers for it to pass, but that it could also result in bad press for the city, so tried to pull it. The motion still had to be voted on, and, after squabbling among themselves in the meeting, the leader of the council told the Labour members to abstain. For some people, it was politics – me being lord mayor was too much airtime, but some of them were being downright spiteful and trying to pooh-pooh everything I did. Challenging the status quo was seen as dangerous, and they viewed me as someone who had to be stopped.

With everything that was happening, I never felt secure in my role. Thankfully, I had the support of so many people in Sheffield, like the creative industries, universities, charities, the youth and people who could see the value in what I was doing. Those are the people who had my back. I also kept saying reminding myself, 'In 12 months' time, are you really going to give a shit what some of these people are whispering about you in the council chamber?'

Meanwhile, as a city, we were making headlines that weren't just associated with aspects of Sheffield's tragic past, like Hillsborough, Orgreave, the sexual exploitation of children or the city's trees being chopped down. So many more people, and especially young people, were engaging in politics, and we were gaining positive press attention for the city – people were genuinely excited about someone who was doing things in a different way. Most of the civil servants at the town hall were supportive, but most of the councillors weren't. They hated having to admit that good things were happening because Sheffield was in the spotlight. Some of them were negative about some of my initiatives at the time but have since altered their opinions and now tell me that they admired some of the things I did.

* * *

As I mentioned earlier, I caused a bit of a stir with a particular tweet after one of my monthly photo campaigns. The tweet, on 4 July 2018, was accompanied by a photo of me wearing a sombrero that had been given to me by the local Mexican community in Sheffield, and a T-shirt bearing the words 'Donald Trump is a wasteman'.

What I wore for my monthly photo campaigns was what I'd wear to chair the subsequent full council meeting, so as you might imagine, I was absolutely bricking it as I walked into the council chamber. My macebearer Julie walked slightly ahead of me into the chamber and cried out the standard refrain of 'Please be upstanding for his right worshipful, the first citizen, Lord Mayor of Sheffield, Councillor Magid Magid.' I walked nervously to the lord mayor's seat, where an attendant was ready to pull it out for me. Then I turned my microphone on and said, 'Please be seated,' before proceeding to the first order of business. But as soon as I'd finished going through the formalities, a Labour councillor stood up to make a point of order, telling me that I was 'bang out of order' to call Donald Trump a wasteman and that I should remove the tweet and apologise. This was followed by some chattering in the chamber, while the chief executive of the council privately told me that not only had every major national broadcast news outlet requested a quote but also that the managing director of Boeing, which was soon to open its first manufacturing site outside the US in Sheffield, had got in touch to say he was disappointed.

Banning Trump was a light-hearted stunt, but in many ways I was absolutely serious. We cannot hold hands with the far right and those who embolden them as the current Conservative government does. Trump, and the politics he represents, threatens the very existence of minorities, which in turn threatens global security and the future of our planet! Just look at his and our government's support for the continued injustice in Palestine and Yemen. We're all familiar with the archaic and destructive industries Trump has bolstered, and his attitude to climate agreements. While our government was preparing to roll out the red carpet for his visit to the UK the following week, I wanted to send the message that Sheffield, a culturally rich city that welcomes and celebrates people of all backgrounds, didn't agree with our government's decision.

Did I think it would have the impact it did? Absolutely not. But before I knew it, the phrase 'Donald Trump is a wasteman' went viral. It was plastered all over London in preparation of his visit, people were selling T-shirts printed with the slogan and I found myself answering questions on CNN and from Jon Snow on *Channel 4 News* about why rolling out the red carpet for Trump was not only ridiculous but dangerous, as it legitimised everything he stands for. Calling him a 'wasteman' was a deliberate tactic. Most importantly, it was accurate, but because the BBC would have to define 'wasteman' on live TV, it would become a talking point. Let's be honest, Trump was never going to visit Sheffield in the first place, but my ban resonated with people as a symbolic gesture. I think I showed the courage that people wanted in their elected leaders who were afraid to take him to task.

Far too many people in politics fail to really connect with people. Some of them merely pretend to, while others make no bones about their lack of interest in the citizens they represent, preferring to advance the party or class to which they belong. I developed some interesting ways of engaging with the people I represented, from inviting the public to watch *Mamma Mia* 2 with me at a local independent cinema to surprising people by joining them in their New Year's celebrations and engaging with them on social media. As tiring as it has been, it has also been really important for me to have been as accessible as possible. For the vast majority of other elected officials, politics is about pursuing power and withholding it from those who are not like them. Wasteman-in-chief Donald Trump is the embodiment of this type of politics: he is more dedicated to his own ego, wealth and racial supremacy than to any single political principle or moral value. He appears to engage with people, but doesn't really care about anyone apart from himself. Other leaders do this less visibly, but they follow the same MO.

* * *

I think one of the reasons I've gathered so much attention over the last year or so is because of a failure in our democracy. The people in power, whether in local or national government, are meant to lead us, but they just don't reflect the people they represent. If we had more women, more people from the LGBT+ community and more people of colour in our politics, it wouldn't be such a surprise that someone like me got to where I have. Even more importantly, I reckon we'd have a much better chance of convincing our elected representatives to take the necessary action to save our collective future. But sometimes you need to take matters into your own hands, and that's one of the reasons why, when Green Party activist Julia Brown tweeted me on 19 March 2019 to say that nominations were out for the elections to the European Parliament in May, I put myself forward as a candidate for the Yorkshire and the Humber region.

With everything that is happening in the world, I couldn't help but ask myself: what the future of Britain was going to be? Who was going to build it? And for the sake of everything I love I refused to believe or accept that it would be people like Boris Johnson and Nigel Farage. I believed (and still believe) there was and is a better story to be told of Britain. One of bringing people together, of hope, and of tolerance. And I wanted to play a role in that.

It seemed fitting that it had been the rise of UKIP in 2014 that got me into politics, and I now had the chance to challenge them head-on. I gained the highest number of votes in the Green Party's selection process for Yorkshire and the Humber and became their lead candidate, with my friend Alison Teal as my running mate.[3] I threw myself into it, and decided to go on a tour around the region, which I

---

[3] The UK's elections to the European Parliament operated a 'regional list' system. Parties usually conduct an internal vote to determine the order that candidates appear on the list. At the election, each person's vote is for the list of candidates who have been chosen to represent the party rather than for a specific candidate. A party gets seats roughly in proportion to the total votes.

gave the fitting European name the 'Tour de Magid'. I handed out leaflets at train stations across Yorkshire, spoke at events and engaged with as many people as I could on the campaign trail, ate a lot of flapjack and custard and managed to fall over on the way to cast my vote – we can blame that one on enthusiasm. And before I knew it, the results were in. I couldn't see them on the big board because I didn't have my glasses on, but my friend Mohammed Bux told me that we'd come second in Sheffield, narrowly losing out to the Brexit Party. But we had beaten Labour (who run the city) and the Lib Dems (the main opposition) by more than 10,000 votes.

The Sheffield result meant a great deal to me, because the Green Party only had a fraction of the resources of the main establishment parties in the city. It filled me with pride and was also a testament to my support there. We came fourth overall in the Yorkshire and the Humber region, with 166,980 votes (over 50 per cent more votes than at the previous election), 13 per cent of the vote. This was enough to win us one of the region's six seats in the European Parliament, which would be allocated to me because I was at the top of the party's list. I needed to put together a speech again, pronto – the Brexit Party may have won the election, but it was the first time a Green MEP had been elected to represent Yorkshire and the Humber and a historic moment; ten years ago, they had elected a BNP MEP. It had been a heroic team effort and I was hugely thankful to everyone that had made it possible, especially my campaign manager, Louise Houghton.

As an MEP, I found myself needing to recruit staff for the first time. Unlike MPs in the House of Commons, all MEPs in the European Parliament play a role in writing legislation and so I needed a policy advisor. I sat on two committees; Civil Liberties, Justice & Home Affairs and Culture & Education. My main areas of focus were migration, discrimination and creative culture. I hadn't advertised anywhere but a lot of people who were looking for jobs with MEPs knew that I was new, so I found myself bombarded with CVs.

Then one night at 10:45pm, me and my chief of staff Abdi were still in the office when I received an email from someone called Silvia Carta. An intern at the UN High Commissioner for Refugees, she was interested. She was a straight-A student who was passionate about changing migration policy and also had a sincere commitment to equality, human rights and social justice. So after a long interview, which was more like an informal chat, I made her my head of policy. Some might say I was naive or that I should have chosen someone with more experience, but I could tell that Silvia was a special talent. She dived right in, picking things up quickly and adapting to situations as they arose. I kept throwing increasingly difficult tasks her way, and she dealt with them so impressively that she's now managing an intern herself. I think the key was giving her space and ownership of her job. She took everything as an opportunity to develop, but always seemed to have my best interests at heart and made me a better MEP as a result. The feeling of investing in someone and seeing them flourish was better than I'd ever expected. Silvia taught me that you should want to hire people who are better than you but also who bring value to whatever it is you're working on. Her passion is so inspiring – it invigorates me and reminds me of why I love what I do.

When I was hiring a media coordinator, we took out an advert that made it clear this could be a temporary position – no one knew what was going to happen in the general election of December 2019 – but to my surprise I ended up getting over 200 applications. I gave the job to a young Scottish woman called Rosie Birchard, who was working at the European Commission. The fact that she would choose to leave a secure job to come and work for me in such insecure circumstances told me she was not only courageous but also relished a challenge. She told me she loved what I did and wanted to have more of a direct influence and be more creative, which was not possible in the Commission. Rosie put together a video application to highlight the skills that she thought I needed, and even started playing a violin halfway through to emphasise some of her USPs! I wanted someone who was good with words and could think creatively, and wow, did she tick those boxes! Her application appealed to me because it was so unique – I suppose it reminded me of how I approach an application. I'm always thinking: 'What's the 99 per cent going to do, and what can I do that's different?'

There were seven people in my office, including me, and what brings us all together is that we want to change the world. I made the choice not to hire anyone who'd worked in the European Parliament before, because I wanted people to come with a fresh perspective and was keen to give opportunities to individuals who had not already had the chance to work there. I thought it was telling that the only two MEP staffers who wore religious headscarves in the entire European Parliament worked in my team. One of my priorities when I was interviewing was asking people what they wanted from the job and how they wanted to develop. As well as guiding my staff members, I wanted them to gain from the experience, feel valued and get the sense that they were developing as people. When you hire someone, you can never be 100 per cent certain about them, because anyone can write one banging cover letter and CV, and perform well at interview. You do your due diligence, but ultimately you have to go with your gut feeling. For me, the most important question that I ask myself is 'Do they care?'

When it comes to ideas in our office, there's a lot of trial and error, and the vast majority don't get off the ground – but some do, and people notice them. There's no formula to it – we'll just throw ideas around and see what sticks. I want to encourage creativity, so even if an idea isn't right, I make a point of rewarding it – there's a chance that the first, second and third idea might be terrible, but the fourth one could be incredible and you don't want to kill off the passion prematurely. I've worked on establishing what makes each of my staff tick, sometimes by giving them some tasks when they start the job that just help me understand them better. One thing that I only realised when a friend pointed it out is that I wasn't praising people enough. I guess that's because I don't like to be praised myself, but since then I've been quite conscious of it.

After the Brexit Bill passed on Thursday 20 December 2019, I went back to work the next day. If the UK leaving the EU wasn't heart-breaking enough, the realisation that we would no longer be working together was devastating, and it moved many of us to tears. The impact of Brexit will be an estimated £130 billion in lost GDP growth over the next 15 years, making people on average £2,250 a year poorer by 2034 – and vulnerable people who need that money most will be disproportionately affected. It makes me so frustrated that the older generation doesn't seem to care about younger people and the world they'll inherit.

*   *   *

I can never be happy with the status quo unless it's benefiting the many. If it's only serving the privileged few, even if I happen to somehow be part of that small bracket myself. I'll always be fighting on the side of justice.

I often hear about working-class people who end up doing well career-wise and rising to the top tier of earners, end up voting Conservative and suddenly wanting to protect the status quo. I feel the same way about these people as I do about immigrants who want to close the door on others. They've been given a ladder but then want to pull it up so no one else can get up – it's selfish, to say the least.

I can accept that some people have shit principles, but if their ideas are being turned into actions, then it should not go unchallenged. And if we haven't got the arguments, let's educate ourselves, read more, equip ourselves and come back. So long as there is dialogue, there is hope. The worry is when people think they know everything and aren't willing to learn. The worst is when people know they're wrong, but their ego gets in the way of them admitting that. I feel like everyone should be a student for life and strive for more knowledge and truth, even if they think they know the truth already. It seems like young people understand this best of all, and it heartens me that so many of them are now so well-informed and politically engaged. But they desperately want change and recognise that we can't keep doing the same things and expecting the results to be different.

That is why we must fill the political elite's vacuum of ideas with our progressive plans and principled solutions for a fairer society. Change for the better is not only *possible* when we come together for the sake of our common prosperity – it is *probable*. With conviction in our beliefs and committed action, with unity, strength and compassion, we will build a world that truly works for everyone.

Inspired by the philosophy of 'doing things differently', I have attempted to use my platform to celebrate Sheffield, to draw awareness to important causes and to bring people together in a world that is trying to drive us apart. The reception – whether on social media, walking through the streets of Sheffield, visiting local schools and businesses or attending events around the country and in Europe, has been overwhelmingly positive and empowering. The status quo has left the majority tired, despairing and wanting something new.

The truth is that the political establishment is not representative of our society – it's out of ideas, out of touch, and out of time. As lord mayor, I always pushed myself to speak out against injustice, standing against racism, hate and intolerance and defending the most disenfranchised sections of our society. In each of my monthly campaigns – whether I was banning Donald Trump while the government rolled out the red carpet for him, challenging Boris Johnson's bigotry, demanding justice from Sajid Javid for the Battle of Orgreave, appointing Sheffield's first poet laureate, launching a UK-wide Suicide Prevention Charter, defending migrants, calling for action on the climate crisis or making the case for an anti-war government – I wore my heart on my sleeve, and the writing is on the T-shirt. My squat became a symbol of defiance. It's up to us to create our own traditions and not conform to standards created by others for themselves. We must get off our high horses, widen levels of engagement and make politics fit for the 21st century.

Every single one of us has some form of platform, some degree of influence. Speaking truth to power and acting according to our capability and opportunity, whatever that may be, is our collective responsibility. Within the fight for a better world, there is space for every one of us to help make that a reality with an activism fuelled by compassion, in charity, politics or protest. We can do things differently.

DO IT DIFFERENTLY

Doing things differently can be scary, and there are people who will hate you for it, but there are also people who will love you for it and want to join you. You might even change the world, in small or large ways, or spark others to do so. But if you keep doing things how they've always been done and sticking to outdated traditions, you risk never knowing what it's like to succeed. So let us make a promise, to not denigrate but to inspire. Rather than bemoan the present, let's paint a picture of what might be. Instead of inciting hatred and instilling fear, let's rise above the chorus of our age and dare to sing a different song.

VII
ALWAYS BUY YOUR ROUND

'Empathy is not simply a matter of trying to imagine what others are going through, but having the will to muster enough courage to do something about it. In a way, empathy is predicated upon hope.'

Cornel West

I know what you're thinking: this chapter title is a bit odd for a Muslim, but it's not solely for religious reasons that I don't drink – it's just never been something I've been that interested in. Even so, 'Always Buy Your Round' is a philosophy that I absolutely swear by. And while it's a simple enough principle, it also taps into values that are important to me: friendship, fairness, empathy, unselfishness, sharing experiences and seeing the bigger picture. That's what 'Always Buy Your Round' means to me.

I've always been curious about other people's lives, ever since I'd take bus trips around the city, overhearing strangers' weird and wonderful conversations. Eventually, as you know, I plucked up the courage to start up conversations with people around me. When I meet people for the first time now, I always try to establish a meaningful connection by asking them something like 'What are you excited about at the moment?' or 'What are you most grateful for in your life?' Just asking a question like that sidesteps any small talk and allows people to open up. Nothing annoys me more than someone asking 'What do you do?' It's such a hollow question. People sometimes ask it as a way of establishing certain things about you without asking you directly, like what social class you're from and how much you earn. I'd rather get on to the things that make a person's eyes light up when they talk about them, and that can be anything from jiu-jitsu to Jenga. If you follow a similar principle, you'll find that people will repay your effort and take a genuine interest in you.

Maybe I take the confidence that it takes to make such an opening gambit for granted. And sure, on rare occasions people might not take kindly to being asked such a question, but I think you should take the risk. I've always felt comfortable talking to people randomly, and you get used to doing it if you spend any time travelling by yourself. I didn't know anyone in Tanzania or Brazil before I went there – I owed so much to the kindness of strangers, who let me sleep on their sofas and showed me the things that they were passionate about, whether that was a library or a Lebanese takeaway joint. I love to see the things that people are passionate about, and it can take you way off the beaten track. Wherever I've been when travelling abroad, I've always been made to feel welcome by my hosts, and I've done the same for people who have found themselves in Sheffield. You end up meeting some of the most extraordinary people – I've collected so many stories from people I've met, and it's an important part of who I am.

ALWAYS BUY YOUR ROUND

This brings me to my golden rule of friendship: always try to take a genuine interest in other people and make them feel good about your interactions. Listen actively rather than passively, and make an effort to let the person know they're being heard. We all have some level of emotional intelligence – if you do find doing this difficult, try using empathetic statements or non-verbal encouragement to reinforce what a person is telling you. The idea of reciprocation is important – doing favours for people and providing them with support makes them feel good, and it's human nature to want to repay the kindness. I'm guilty of not practicing what I preach here, but I'm still learning. I'm crap at taking compliments – I just don't know how to react to them and am far more comfortable dealing with constructive criticism. I'm also not good at opening up to friends about how I'm feeling; I'll tell them everything's fine, when that's sometimes far from true. I remember getting in a rut as a kid and not wanting to involve anyone else in it, and I still feel that way to a certain extent, like I'll be able to pull myself out of whatever issue I'm dealing with. Part of that stems from not wanting to drag anyone else down, I suppose. I know it helps to talk about your problems, but sometimes I just can't take my own advice. But I have learned to be more compassionate towards myself.

Sometimes you can be unaware how much a compliment or the act of asking a simple question can mean to someone, as my regular bus journeys with Delores proved. Your life can be enriched so much by what might start out as a brief conversation. You never know what you're going to learn or where you might end up when you decide to engage with someone, rather than just keep your head down and carry on walking. And random acts of kindness can be such a powerful force for good.

One particularly random act came after the comedian Rufus Hound, who I'd never met, sent me a Twitter message while I was lord mayor in July 2018, to tell me that he was in Sheffield and asked if I'd like to hang out. I was quite baffled that someone I'd frequently seen on TV and admired would reach out like that. After a brief burst of excitedly messaging my friends about it, I had to think of something interesting to do. It was the day after England's defeat against Croatia in the World Cup semi-final and it seemed like the whole country was in mourning, so I came up with an idea to cheer people up. We did a shout-out on Twitter and asked if anyone in Sheffield wanted us to come to their offices with some treats. We started out with buckets of Haribo but those went pretty quickly, so it evolved into a completely random selection of treats that included lottery scratchcards, wet wipes and pet food. People picked out what they wanted, and one girl won £50 on a scratchcard!

* * *

I would not be where I am today without the kindness and sacrifices made by my family, friends, volunteers, supporters and well-wishers. In turn, I've always felt it would be selfish not to help other people to come up too. That's why I worked hard to encourage some remarkable people during my time as lord mayor, like Kaltum and Angela. I knew they would become terrific Sheffield city councillors, and they are both doing incredible work in their wards.

I also selected five young people aged between 18 and 25, who had got in touch to say that they saw me as a role model and wanted to get into politics. It wasn't an official mentoring programme, but I met up with them several times, chatted to them on social media and have kept in touch. I wasn't telling them what to do but rather listening as they told me where they wanted to get to and trying to find ways to support them. It was varied work: sometimes I'd need to challenge them, sometimes I'd need to support them by guiding them towards literature and figures who had inspired me, and at other times it would be a case of using the contacts I'd made to help them gain work experience. One of them shared my goals, so I actually ended up employing him, and still do to this day. So be brave enough to send that email, and be politely persistent. I'm reminded of the time that I contacted Natalie Bennett, then leader of the Green Party, when I was thinking of joining them, and she responded straight away. Passion and enthusiasm can be both inspiring and infectious.

Growing up in a socially deprived community like I did, I've seen people go down paths I wish they hadn't. But we were more fortunate than kids today because we had youth clubs, which offered a safe haven. It was amazing to have a place to go with cheap food and drink, games of football and people who seemed to give a shit about you, but youth clubs were much more than this. They were also a gateway to opportunities, particularly for underprivileged kids from disadvantaged backgrounds. They also stopped a lot of vulnerable teenagers getting caught up in gangs. I feel massively grateful to my local youth club in Burngreave, but there are no longer any council-funded youth clubs in my ward – it's these places that have found themselves at the sharp end of the austerity cuts. The misery created by Tory austerity over the past decade is proof that without these values of fairness, empathy and unselfishness, society can become very ugly indeed.

With each newsflash of another young life lost to violence on the streets, I'm reminded of people I grew up with who had their lives savagely taken from them way too early – young people full of unrealised potential and unfulfilled dreams. In 2018 there were more than 40,000 offences involving knives in England and Wales – the highest number since 2011, with over 280 victims dying from stabbings. I'll never forget being called and told that one of my constituents, a young, talented student named Fahim Hersi, had been stabbed to death outside a Sheffield cinema. It sent shockwaves throughout the community. Visiting his mother the next day to convey my sympathies, and seeing her grief and despair is something that will stay with me forever, and it's not something I ever want to do again.

Tragic deaths like Fahim's are entirely preventable – they're the inevitable consequence of widespread systemic dysfunction and wilful ignorance within this Tory government's institutionally short-sighted policies. The media often paint the problem as a 'race issue' or a crisis within the black community, but it's actually a crisis of deprivation, of few opportunities, dangerous environments and no alternatives. A crisis of insufficient investment in our education system and the dismantling of youth services across the country.

Yes, young black men are disproportionately more likely to be unemployed or found in prisons, in failing schools and in child poverty. A series of overlapping disadvantages further compounded by year after year of disastrous Tory policy, with cuts across the board. In London, the statistics show that most of the victims and suspects of knife crime are black (victims 44 per cent, suspects 48 per cent), but for the rest of the UK they are overwhelmingly white (victims 89 per cent, suspects 81 per cent). The truth is that this is a problem that affects all of us.

Safety in our communities has been knowingly threatened by politicians who cut away at community police numbers, local government budgets and services for young people. Research by the YMCA has found that funding for youth services across England has fallen by £737 million or 62 per cent, since the Tories came into power in 2010. Hundreds of youth centres have closed, thousands of youth workers have lost their jobs and more than 100,000 places for young people have vanished into thin air. Austerity has helped breed a negative environment and a lost generation of kids, who feel abandoned by the state. We should be committing to helping young people make the right choices, and to making them feel nurtured and supported – that way, the whole community will rise together. Priti and Boris, it's time to stop the cuts, increase investment and watch the violent incidents tumble.

Pseudo-solutions that are deeply mired in historical racial prejudice, like criminalising drill music, ramping up stop and search or increasing the number of incarcerations isn't going to solve the wave of knife crime, and nor is charity a permanent solution – we are in need of a concrete and radical upheaval of our social policy. There must be a genuine commitment to deal with the extensive fear of crime that permeates our communities and is the primary reason why young people carry knives in the first place. We must do more to improve the social conditions that are fertile grounds for weapon possession.

To the young men who feel the need to carry knives – I understand your fear. Hope has been torn from you, your safety has been neglected and the future seems bleak. But while I, and many others, continue to push the government to commit to proper solutions for the mess that has been imposed on you, please leave the knife at home. It's just not worth it – the loss of a single young person is painful for each and every one of us. The government are in denial, and they will point fingers in any direction instead of admitting culpability. We must keep speaking up, speaking out and fighting until the deadly cuts are reversed. Until every young person in this country is safe.

One person who does speak out and fight every day is Safiya Saeed, a community leader from Burngreave in Sheffield, where I grew up. She founded a community group called Big Brother Burngreave, which brings together boys of all backgrounds to use their time positively. While its main focus is sport, it also provides a mentoring programme, with specialists coming in to talk about gang culture, knife crime and mental health. Sport Relief initially provided the funding and training for community groups like this. While Safiya established the group, it is now run by its teenage members. To mark the success of the project at the end of its first year, I invited some of the boys and organisers to the town hall to acknowledge their effort, putting on an evening of celebration with music, food, dancing and speeches, letting them try on my cloak and chain and hold my mace. I was a kid just like them, and it only takes one spark.

I've been fortunate enough to be able to give something back to my community, and one charity is especially close to my heart. The Unity Gym Project was founded in Broomhall, which is in the ward I used to represent, in 2010 by a guy called Saeed Brasab. I had the privilege of working with Saeed during my term as lord mayor, and he knows first-hand the struggles facing young boys in the community. The amazing thing about Saeed and his project is that it's all volunteer-led, which makes you wonder how great an impact they would be having if it was properly funded. First and foremost, the Unity Gym is a place that helps young people make positive life choices. It's such an important centre in the community and in addition to a gym provides a host of other services, like helping young people develop life skills through mentoring placements, organising trips and events, providing activities during the school holidays and mediators to improve cohesion in the community. Perhaps most importantly, though, it's a safe space for kids to come to.

Giving a spotlight to community organisations and smaller charities really makes a difference, and I did as much as I could to help them while I was lord mayor. For Unity Gym, I'd organise and front fundraising events, set up meetings with council officers, direct them to funding pots, mention them on social media or in newspaper articles and would wear branded T-shirts and hoodies to interviews – as many things as I could think of to raise their profile and support them. As lord mayor, you're asked to nominate three charities, which donations from various individuals and organisations are shared between. Along with Unity Gym, I chose Sheffield Women's Counselling and Therapy Service (now called Saffron), a free therapy and counselling service for women who have suffered abuse and trauma, and Sheffield Flourish, a community mental health charity that works collaboratively to build innovative digital and community projects.

* * *

Promoting positive mental health is very important to me, which is why I conceived the UK's first Suicide Prevention Charter. Suicide is the biggest killer of men under the age of 45, but many of us don't realise how common it is. I'm no mental health expert, but I do know that more than 6,000 people commit suicide every year in the UK. According to the World Health Organization, the worldwide figure is more than 800,000 people, and we must do something about it. I decided to launch the charter on 10 July 2018, as part of World Suicide Prevention Day. Mental health affects everyone, regardless of background, and the aim of this campaign is to get as many organisations across the country to pledge to create or enhance policies that will improve the mental health of their members. We want to send out a message that more can be done to prevent suicide by encouraging as many people as possible to take the pledge and take that step further.

There are many risk factors that can lead to suicide, such as mental health problems, bullying, trauma, abuse and even socio-economic problems such as unemployment. Sometimes there are obvious signs that someone is feeling suicidal, but that isn't always the case. If you are suffering yourself, it can be hard to realise this and seek treatment, but it's crucial that you get help. Above all, remember that the feeling will pass and that you will get better. The pain is real, but so is hope!

I know personally that a simple message to someone who is struggling can literally save their life. A colleague of mine seemed to go, all of a sudden, from being as happy as Larry and always telling terrible jokes into a deeply sad recluse. Although I wasn't as close to him as other colleagues were, something told me that things weren't right. When I asked people if they thought he was ok, they'd reply with, 'He'll be alright – he's probably just not feeling well.' Two weeks went by and he was still the same, so I dropped him an email. I knew he was a keen runner and had a marathon coming up, so I asked him for some running tips.

He was reluctant at first but thankfully said yes, so we arranged to meet up after work for a hot chocolate. When I asked him if he was alright, he just burst out crying and everything came out suddenly, as if he'd been bottling it all up for some time. He told me he was having financial problems and felt hopeless and suicidal. I did my best to support him by pointing him in the direction of professionals who could help, as well as just being there for him and listening to his problems. So if you know of anyone who might be feeling down or has been talking about suicide, threatening to hurt themselves, suffering from mood changes, isolating themselves or feeling like they're a burden to others, please just reach out to them. Send them a message asking if they're ok, letting them know you're there and that it's important to talk. Just remember to listen, not to judge and to be compassionate.

We need to break the silence and have each other's backs, because we are living in a society where stigma keeps people from seeking help and stops others from even talking about it. We seriously need to change the culture around mental health, look out for one another and show compassion.

* * *

It's no secret that I'm a proud Europhile and still advocate for the United Kingdom to remain in the EU. However, like many people, I recognise that the EU is in need of serious reform. And much to the chagrin of some, I've been publicly critical of the conventions of the European Union, its legislators and its officials. Even though I don't believe the EU is always a safe haven for progressive ideas, my belief in the EU project – its historic necessity, present value and unrealised potential – has not wavered in the slightest during my time as an MEP. But while I praise its fundamental goals, I don't believe that the current set up of the EU is going to achieve them. For a truly cohesive, thriving Europe, for a Union true to its purpose, to be a continent at the forefront of just, sustainable human progress, there must be a more equitable distribution of prosperity between its member countries and an even-handed sharing of burdens of all kinds.

I once stated that many of the EU's leading voices were avoiding tough choices and conversations. I've seen nothing to convince me otherwise. On the contrary, my experiences have only served to cement this opinion.

While I was highlighting the devastation of child refugees drowning in the Mediterranean in the Strasbourg hemicycle, the vice president who was chairing the discussion thought it apt to attack me for wearing a baseball cap. Weeks later, when I condemned Boris Johnson for his bigotry and disaster-capitalist agenda, calling him as a racist, a liar, a charlatan and a national disgrace — all on very good grounds — I was served a suspension warning by European Parliament President David Sassoli for what he said was 'offensive language'.

I felt a responsibility to the people who put their faith in me at the ballot box – for many of them it was the first time they voted Green. I needed to show that their vote wasn't wasted, so I felt a pressure to do the best I could and fight for change where it's needed. There was also pressure from people I feel like are voiceless – those who aren't championed enough and those who are suffering. Then there were the people who campaigned for me, like Louise Houghton, a fellow Green Party candidate for MEP who became my campaign manager – I didn't want to let them down. Louise stood up for me and even stood *on* me for therapeutic reasons, when my back gave out in the run-up to the election.

When I was elected, I continued to fight with everything I had. I was loud and proud, unapologetic in my support for positive, progressive values. We were emboldened by the 'Green Wave' that was cascading through Europe, including an incredible result in Germany, where Green and allied parties won 22 of their 69 seats in the European Parliament. In France, a third-placed finish saw the Europe Écologie-Les Verts party win another seven seats. I'm writing this after our government has taken us out of the EU. It pains me to see Britain relegated to continuing to talk about herself in a room containing ever fewer friends. While nothing can make this spectacle easier to witness, the good news is that the Greens are becoming a major political force in Europe. There is some hope ahead, even if it is not on British shores.

I hoped as a party we could lead the efforts to stop turning a blind eye to preventable tragedies in the Mediterranean, where the door is slammed firmly shut in the faces of migrants, refugees and asylum seekers who flee their homes and are desperate for safety. As a refugee who was resettled in a welcoming place like Sheffield, I feel that it is my duty to help other people who are in similar situations.

During a heart-wrenching trip organised by a charity called Refugee Rights Europe, I travelled to the French-Italian border, where the human rights of refugees and migrants have been violated every day since 2015. I saw refugees and displaced people of all ages and from all corners of the planet who had fled poverty, persecution, war, ecological breakdown and had undergone unimaginably traumatic journeys. Many of them had been dehumanised, demeaned and treated with disdain. There is irrefutable evidence that these vulnerable people, including innocent, unaccompanied, asylum-seeking children, have suffered pushbacks – indeed, I've witnessed it myself. I've seen scandalous goings-on, with border police falsely recording dates of birth on documents to refuse entry, and also confiscating birth certificates. These examples represent a remorseless neglect of universal human rights and the wanton abuse of European law.

The time for minced words, mild manners and tedious tinkering over a system doomed to fail is over. For real change, this is what I call on the EU to do:

Firstly, the EU institutions must at the very least deliver on their pledge to resettle 50,000 migrants – a number that represents just 1.6 per cent of global need. If people are drowning in the Mediterranean, don't stand by and watch from your gilded tower. Refugees and migrants are the manifestation of human perseverance and belief that there can be a better life. Treat them as you would like to be treated.

Secondly, to the College of Commissioners, I demand real action against the overwhelming tide of anti-Muslim racism flowing from hateful headlines and bigoted politicians' words and seeping into the pores of our society. Now that the U.K. has left, the number of Muslim-identifying MEPs and people of colour keeps shrinking. The EU cannot continue to avoid uncomfortable conversations on race and discrimination. It's simple: the EU's management machine no longer represents the reality of the continent's increasingly vibrant, diverse, multi-ethnic, multi-religious and multiracial societies. To truly connect with all European citizens and to inspire and motivate them, EU institutions must look like the societies they represent.

Lastly, the EU must wake up to the harsh reality that the world before us is going up in flames. Whether we like it or not, whether we wish to escape it or brainlessly deny the science behind it, we are the first generation armed with the knowledge that human action is propelling life on our planet toward the brink of collapse. This leaves us with the opportunity and obligation to decide on the continuing habitability of our planet for all species. While a European Green Deal holds tremendous hope and promise, it does not go nearly far enough.

During my time in the European Parliament, I joined forces with MEPs who were embarking on similar struggles and became a co-president of the European Parliament Anti-Racism and Diversity Intergroup. The group performs vital work that promotes racial equality, opposes racism and educates about the importance of non-discrimination in the work of the European Parliament. I worked with good people like Romeo Franz, a German MEP and member of the European Green Party who defends the rights of the Romani population across Europe. It surprised me to learn that there was no tradition of having Friday prayers in the European Parliament, as there are many Muslims in the parliament buildings in Brussels and Strasbourg. After some wrangling, on 24 January 2020 we hosted the first ever Jumu'ah prayer and welcomed 70 people of many faiths, beliefs and backgrounds. This was a beautiful moment of human unity, and I'm proud that these prayers continue to be held every Friday.

I owe a great deal to the people who have come with me on my journey in the European Parliament, from the great staff who worked there that always had my back, to fellow colleagues like British Green MEP Alex Phillips and Mohammed Chahim, a Dutch-Moroccan MEP from the Socialist group who I'm still good friends with, and of course the young people who worked in my office. I've always thought that the more you invest in people, the more they will give back in return. I've worked hard to make sure my team feels appreciated, nurtured and challenged, encouraging them take more risks and be more confident and creative.

Sadly, when the Tories emerged from the general election in December 2019 with a large majority, Brexit became an inevitability. This meant that I'd have to disband my team, so I made it a priority to support them in finding new roles. Three of them are now currently working in three different parliaments: the European Parliament, British Parliament and the Republic of Ireland parliament; others are working in media or the private sector. Working with this dream team for just a short time has taught me a lot about the next generation of activists and given me so much hope for what they're going to achieve.

The fate of British MEPs may have been sealed by Brexit, but the script of what is to come has not yet been written. The fight for a better world doesn't end with a referendum, a general election or the ratification of the withdrawal agreement in the

European Parliament. Now, more than ever, we must stick together, hold this government to account and make sure the most vulnerable citizens are protected. The path will be arduous, but there is cause for optimism: an emboldened younger generation is fostering a new consensus and developing a political will to deliver transformative change. And who knows – perhaps I'll be back in Brussels one day, with a few more grey hairs and propelled by a campaign of hope.

The EU is not a perfect institution – but at its core, it espouses values of fairness, community and togetherness. These are values which bind society together and remind us of our common humanity.

VIII
DON'T KISS A TORY

'You're not to be so blind with patriotism that you can't face reality. Wrong is wrong, no matter who does it or says it.'

Malcolm X

Full disclaimer: this is my 'standing on a soapbox' chapter. If I get really animated, it's just because I care about this stuff so much, and some of it really pisses me off. And if you don't agree with me, at least it'll spark a conversation! As long as we can keep talking, that has to be something, even if we disagree.

I can honestly say that I've never kissed a Tory – well, not knowingly, anyway. And if I ever did, there's nothing a bit of disinfectant can't remedy. Just kidding! Maybe. Anyway, I didn't think that this 'commandment' was going to attract the attention and initiate the uproar that it did, and I certainly didn't expect *BBC News* to dedicate a segment to it. It was hilarious to see high-profile journalists interviewing Sheffielders outside our town hall, asking them whether they thought it was appropriate for me to command others not to kiss Tories. Some people genuinely asked if I was instructing them not to kiss their Tory mothers, while others were vowing that they wouldn't be spending their money in Sheffield anymore. A few even threatened legal action, although the grounds for that were obviously dubious. Of course, the 'commandment' was tongue-in-cheek – I wasn't seriously intending to police the streets for signs of romantic relations that transgressed party lines!

The interest generated recalled the 'Never Kissed a Tory' tagline that LGBT+ Labour introduced in 2008. Their co-chair, the Hackney councillor Katie Hanson, explained that it was just a light-hearted stunt and 'more of an aspiration . . . it does not have to be true for you to buy the T-shirt!' The slogan was an instant marketing success, appearing on posters, T-shirts and mugs, helping to promote what became a lucrative fundraising campaign. And yet, there was also a backlash of sorts. As Owen Jones, the prominent left-wing socialist journalist, was quick to quip in response to the furore: 'Always amusing how the right accuses the left of being perpetually offended by everything, yet this light-hearted message about kissing has left a load of right-wingers frothing at the mouth.' Several years later, LGBT+ Conservatives designed a counter-campaign with 'I Kissed a Tory, and I Liked it'. Maybe they do have a sense of humour after all.

I appreciate that the political discourse in recent years has become increasingly bitter, so my commandment probably pissed more people off than it would have done previously. All my other commandments speak to universal values, so why did I choose to be explicitly political with this one? Well, it's partly because I believe the Tories have been responsible for waging a war on the most vulnerable people in society, through the devastating and unnecessary years of austerity. I can't hide how I feel the world should be, and it's not a place with a Tory government at the helm.

As a black, Muslim refugee, my experience in life has led me down the path of fighting injustice on behalf of others. This is always underlined by my belief above all else that immigrants make Britain great. However, right now, in this country, some from immigrant backgrounds occupy influential positions in the corridors of power and yet are intent on heartlessly slamming the door shut to others, denying people opportunities, rendering many of them dispossessed and discarding them to endless cycles of destitution.

For a few years now, the Conservative Party has shamelessly boasted of its abhorrent intention to introduce an 'Australian-style points-based system' for immigration. This would mean a future where people are granted entry according to the 'value' they bring to our country. Not much luck then if you're poor, or if you are a member of a minoritised, underprivileged community. Let's be clear, I believe that regardless of whether Boris Johnson said "colour" or "talent" in one of his many incoherent rambles, the Tory party's 'good migrant' versus 'bad migrant' blueprint for immigration is, in itself, racist. Numerous attempts to sanitise their plans through plastering Sajid Javid, Priti Patel, James Cleverly, Rishi Sunak or any other Conservative of colour on our television screens does nothing to alter this reality.

Patel, the current home secretary, has promised to end the free movement of people once and for all. She is one of a handful of high-profile Tories who seem to think their immigrant backgrounds are a flawless justification for pushing sinister policies that marginalise migrants. There are now self-serving black and brown faces in high places, happy to pander to the far-right through Trumpian laws and anti-immigration rhetoric. Just as they did during their banking and hedge-fund careers, they serve the special interests of the ruling class who offer them a seat at the table, and not the interests of the vilified communities to which they belong.

This straight-talking, working-class, Somali Yorkshireman isn't buying the act. The Australian immigration system is racist, and horrifyingly barbaric. Its offshore detention centres are cages in which their border enforcement officials imprison refugees and asylum seekers. The deeply disturbing situation there is deemed a human rights emergency by Amnesty International. It is nothing to aspire towards; indeed it is a dehumanising system symptomatic of ecofascist, end-stage disaster-capitalism which humanity must unite in denouncing together.

If this is what lies ahead for us in the UK, then there is much to dread for immigrant communities, and those who believe in a fairer, more equal and collaborative society. The notion of meritocracy is a con. Our unrepresentative, structurally racist institutions are cold, hard proof of the duplicitous veneer of a rigged system that rewards existing power and privilege and punishes difference and disadvantage. If meritocracy bolsters the best or allows certain 'corn-flakes to get to the top' as Johnson argued back in 2013, then almost all our best must be entitled, white, rich, Etonian members of the ruling class. That is nonsense – plain and simple.

As an immigrant who has been elected to political positions, I am where I am not because of meritocracy, but thanks to luck and the support of those of us who believe in a compassionate alternative to what the Tories stand for. There are millions just like me who were not afforded opportunity through no fault of their own. They exist in every constituency and every community. Today, we can transform our country in such a way that future generations are not held back by the same, or more cutthroat, discriminatory forces. Daughters, sons, aunts, neighbours, friends of immigrants, and immigrants yourselves – people like me who are elected to represent you must say it loud and clear. Our diversity, our openness and our solidarity is what makes Britain truly great. So let's take our pride and outrage to the ballot box, and let's come together to kick the Conservative Party out of power.

* * *

I'm a product of Sheffield, and 'Don't Kiss a Tory' was intended as a respectful nod to the great Steel City's political past and working-class heritage. That past has been proudly left-wing and profoundly radical. Sometimes, the rabble-rousing radicals of yesterday – like those crazy folk who wanted to abolish slavery, give women the vote and put an end to racial segregation – become the lawmakers of tomorrow.

Between 1787 and 1794, a Sheffield journalist called Joseph Gales published the radical newspaper the *Sheffield Register*. He expressed support for causes that at the time were regarded as extreme and disruptive, from the abolition of slavery and religious tolerance to questioning the role of monarchs and welcoming scientific advancement. In 1789 he hailed the French Revolution, commending the victory of 'our French brethren over despots'. Two years later, he co-founded the Sheffield Society for Constitutional Information, which sought the reform of parliament, then wholly controlled by the aristocratic elite (what changes!). The society had 2,000 members within a year and was proving a headache for the authorities. Following an attempt by the Duke of Norfolk and Reverend James Wilkinson to enclose 6,000 acres of common land at Stannington and Hallam, rioting ensued and several buildings were set on fire, including Wilkinson's library, with the crowd shouting 'No king' and 'No taxes'. The authorities responded by shutting down the newspaper and constructing emergency barracks to restore order. During centuries of post-industrial human existence, there have been many positive developments, but tactics of repression, censorship, militarisation and the brutality of uniformed security services against working people have remained constant.

The first women's suffrage organisation, the Sheffield Female Political Association, was established in 1851 by Anne Kent, her husband, and Mrs Anne Knight, a prominent campaigner for the abolition of slavery. The group passed a resolution written by Higginbotham in support of enfranchising women, which persuaded the Earl of Carlisle to bring a petition to the House of Lords. While it was received with laughter, it is still a significant milestone in the history of women's suffrage. When you disrupt the status quo and present a more equal vision, you will face laughter, you will receive abuse and everything you propose will likely be dismissed without a moment's consideration. But when the tide of progress inevitably turns, it sweeps away those who stood rooted in the ground. Yesterday's absurd handful are celebrated today as the revolutionary, courageous few.

Among these people was the well-known radical writer Edward Carpenter (1844–1929), for whom Sheffield was also home. He highlighted the terrible working conditions of industrial workers and later became a pioneering advocate for equality, gay rights, trade unions and environmental protection. In September 2019, the 'Friends of Edward Carpenter' group announced that a public sculpture was being created to recognise his historical and social importance to the city.

As recently as the 1980s, Sheffield's left-wing city council earned the city the nickname the 'People's Republic of South Yorkshire'. It became a thorn in the side of Margaret Thatcher's Conservative Government, a bastion of resistance and solidarity. The Red Flag was flown above Sheffield Town Hall under David Blunkett's Labour council on May Day in the 1980s. They also passed motions calling for nuclear disarmament, declaring the local authority a 'nuclear-free zone' in November 1980. 'Peace officers' were employed to promote peace and harmonious international relations, contradicting the council's requirements to implement civil defence plans. In September 1982, in the middle of the Cold War, Sheffield City Council signed a joint peace treaty with the city of Donetsk, which was then in the Ukrainian Soviet Socialist Republic. In 1983, the National Union of Mineworkers relocated its headquarters to Sheffield in the run-up to the miners' strike of 1984–85, and the region became the nucleus for this historically significant collaborative and consequential act of disruption, the repercussions of which are felt to this day.

* * *

For many people, their preferred political party is like a beloved football team – win or lose, and regardless of who the manager is, that's just who they are. It is fundamental to the identity through which they define themselves – it's not really about policies at all. It's rarely based on extensive ideological under-standing or dependent on a list of desires for specific outcomes. I see this across both the green pastures of the rural Tory south and in northern towns, where people almost exclusively state, 'I'm a Labour voter. I couldn't be anything different, else my gran would be rolling in her grave.' It took something as cataclysmic as Brexit for some of our country's most partisan vot-ers to break this mould.

My mum had no family history to guide her behav-iour at the ballot box when we moved to Sheffield from Somalia in 1994. The next year, she voted in the Sheffield City Council Election and chose to support Stephen Jones, the Labour candidate who unseated Independent Labour incumbent James Jamison. We used to get both Labour and Green Party leaflets through the letterbox in the run-up to elections.

Burngreave – the inner-city district I grew up in – was then part of the Brightside and Hillsborough con-stituency. My mum's vote in 1997 helped to re-elect

David Blunkett, Tony Blair's appointment as home secretary, who had by this time lost the radical fire that had fuelled his politics when he was leader of the city council in the 1980s. Throughout the Blair years, my mum came to conclude that in British politics, politicians were untrustworthy whether they were red or blue. They seemed to work to protect the interests of the super-rich and special interests alone, with little ambition to disrupt anything for the better on behalf of us ordinary people.

The year 1997 also saw Princess Diana die in that wretched Parisian tunnel. A countless number of those from immigrant backgrounds had built up a real affinity with her over the years. We were shocked and saddened when the news of her tragic death first broke, and I remember my mum crying in our front room at what felt like a loss for us all. I think it's because she was, quite uniquely, a member of the ruling elite who genuinely connected on a human level with people from ethnic minority cultures. She didn't come across as aristocratic or haughty – she looked like a rebel who wanted to change the world, and she always wore her heart on her sleeve. She didn't marginalise us or look down on us, despite having married into a family that once subjugated our countries of origin to centuries of suffocating colonisation. She was not afraid to carve out her own path. The single greatest act of disruption is often refusing to conform. In an environment that sidelines you for your differences and refusal to play by the rules, sometimes you have to Meghan Markle your way out of there.

Despite growing up with my mum as a Labour supporter, I've never had an ingrained allegiance to any political party – for me, it's all about policies, principles and people. This was evident during last year's general election when I called on the Green Party to stand down in all Labour/Conservative marginal seats after the Brexit Party and the Conservatives formed an unholy hard-right pact. With Farage helping deliver a parliamentary majority for Boris, we were walking into inevitable disaster.

It was a tough call to make but there was just so much at stake. A win for Boris would have meant a victory for oil and gas magnates, greedy pharmaceutical conglomerates and the hedge fund elites, with job security, environmental protections, migrant and workers' rights at great risk. I would have loved for Labour and the Greens to have worked together but despite the Greens attempting this, frustratingly Labour were not willing to even entertain this idea. Sadly, the Greens did join a pact with the austerity peddling Lib Dems and stood down many Green candidates across the country. This strategy unsurprisingly proved to be a disastrous decision for the Greens.

I came into politics due to the rise of UKIP and found my home in the Green movement amongst hardworking courageous friends trying to save our world and make it better for everyone. The thought of waking up to a Tory government, excited to impose 5 more years of misery on the most vulnerable, thinking we could have done more to stop them made me sick to my depths. Even though I got a lot of harsh criticism from Green Party officials and some members, for me it was about doing the right thing and putting the national interest first – with or without being asked. And although not all Green candidates stood down, I know as a result of my call out two candidates did.

* * *

I think I realised in 2010 that my political beliefs were a result of wanting to support the most vulnerable and neglected in society, and of seeing inherent value

THE ART OF DISRUPTION

in everybody. At around the time of the general election in that year, I started reading more about the political parties and their core policies, and it became clear that my deeply held principles were poles apart from both historical Conservative Party agendas and those of the Tories that led the coalition government from May 2010.

David Cameron famously announced, 'We're in this together' at the Tory Party Conference in October 2009, but the next year proved to many of us that nothing could be further from the truth. In 2010, and in a coalition government, freshly post-swine flu outbreak, passionate porcine aficionado Cameron got swiftly to work. Barely a month after taking power, George Osborne's first budget commenced their decade-long, vicious programme of austerity. A massive reduction in public expenditure, combined with tax cuts for the wealthiest and welfare cuts for the poorest, followed. While the rich got richer, communities across the country were devastated, and we hurtled towards entrenched inequality and climate chaos. And when civil unrest began to rise, anger was deflected towards migrants and minorities, and they just carried on.

In March 2010, Cameron said, 'I wouldn't change child benefit, I wouldn't means-test it, I don't think that's a good idea.' But on 7 January 2013, a law was passed that did just that. The same thing happened with educational maintenance allowance – crucial for so many in post-16 education – when it was abruptly scrapped in October 2010. Welfare cut followed welfare cut, energy and water bills were left to spiral, public services were hollowed out and our education was put through a kitchen blender with children left to navigate the resulting mush. A poll of 2,000 headteachers in 2019 revealed that cuts to school budgets since 2012 had resulted in four out of five teachers using their own money to support schoolchildren, with three out of four admitting to relying on contributions from parents to prop up their teaching budgets. Our children will inherit the world around us, so they deserve the space to grow, to learn, to feed their creativity and dream. Instead, they're left hungry and without the resources and support they need to excel. We're not just ignoring them and threatening their futures, we're depriving them of their childhoods.

With the unprecedented surge in homelessness and record levels of in-work poverty, austerity has also caused a mental health crisis. The National Institute for Health Research confirmed that its impact was a contributing factor to the sustained rise in the suicide rate following the economic downturn in 2008 and 2009. In addition to this, a TUC report published in 2018 revealed that there was just one mental health doctor for every 253 patients. In a society where the ability of every human being to thrive was guaranteed, everybody would recognise their own worth. But as public spaces are increasingly commercialised and public services are torn to shreds, with millions living below the breadline, what do we expect? The years of austerity have created a world that keeps many of our fellow human beings in entrenched misery, forced to suffer alone following cuts to support services. This is not a coincidence – it is political. The born-to-rule elite long ago concluded that they must weaken the masses to hinder their capacity to disrupt and their ability to claim fair representation and a share of power.

Dominic Raab, currently the Foreign Secretary, claimed in 2017 that 'the typical user of a foodbank is not someone who's languishing in poverty – it's someone who has a cash flow problem episodically.'[4] Such

---

[4] Dominic Raab made this comment on Victoria Derbyshire's BBC Two show on 29 May 2017, two weeks before he was appointed Minister of State for Courts and Justice.

a mind-boggling lack of empathy can only stem from a background drenched in privilege, far removed from the plight of those in need. The use of foodbanks is growing exponentially: according to the Trussell Trust, the six months between April and September 2019 were the busiest on record. One Tory MP, Miriam Cates, who was among those who broke through Labour's 'red wall' in the December 2019 general election, had previously set up an app called Foodbank in 2014. It charges foodbanks a fee of £180 to list items that are in short supply, so people can make sure they donate products that are most needed. It's hard not to regard this as the predatory exploitation of the poverty and misery of others, and this isn't the leadership our country deserves. Recognising such an absence of humanity in our representatives should make us both angry and sad, and it is these emotions that motivate and encourage acts of political disruption.

My time as lord mayor gave me the platform to show the relevance of politics to people's everyday lives. When good people sit back and refrain from involvement, travesties can happen. I believe politics doesn't belong to the wealthy elite, who are sat in lavish offices on comfy chairs with even comfier bank balances. Nobody is entitled to more than their fair share of power; politics must be made accessible for everyone, and I try to promote that belief in everything I do. Inadequate representation in politics breeds mistrust, while diverse representation builds respect and understanding. And if I'm being honest, one of the many reasons I attracted so much attention as lord mayor is due to a failure of democracy. If we look at the elected officials who claim to lead us, in both local and national government, they do not reflect the people they're meant to represent. Let's look at the current Tory government, the people responsible for running our country and making decisions on our behalf. Out of the current members of the cabinet, 62 per cent were privately educated, and half of them studied at Oxford or Cambridge. The new chancellor, Rishi Sunak, is a former Goldman Sachs banker and the son-in-law of a billionaire. How on earth are these members of the elite going to understand child poverty or empathise with the devastating impact of austerity?

* * *

I learned very early on that you can't expect the wrong people to do the right thing. You will never receive an invitation to the world of representation and power, and no one's going to ask you your choice of entrance music (believe me, I waited!). The establishment tends not to like newcomers, especially ones that don't resemble them. If you want to make a difference, it's up to you to bring your A-game and do what it takes to be heard. And in the present era of 'post-truth politics', this is no easy task. At a time when politicians peddle flagrant lies, painting them on buses and flooding the public sphere with them, with little accountability and no fear of punishment, ordinary people must be heard. When the 2016 Vote Leave campaign said, 'We send the EU £350 million a week – let's fund the NHS instead,' we needed to be more than just angry at their disingenuity. Because lies like this, unchecked and left to fester, can upend the entire political landscape.

Boris continued to stick to this ridiculous figure. Writing in the *Telegraph* on 16 September 2017, he said, 'And yes – once we have settled our accounts, we will take back control of roughly £350 million per week. It would be a fine thing, as many of us have pointed out, if a lot of that money went on the NHS.' Sir David Norgrove, the Chair of the UK Statistics Authority, criticised Johnson for a 'clear misuse of official statistics', pointing out that he had 'confused' the size of the UK's annual gross and net contributions to the EU budget. Everyone's least favourite mop-headed imbecile retorted:

> You say that I claim that there would be £350 million that 'might be available for extra public spending' when we leave the EU. This is a complete misrepresentation of what I said, and I would like you to withdraw it. [What I said] is very different from claiming that there would be an extra £350 million available for public spending, and I am amazed that you should impute such a statement to me.

The selective amnesia of the ruling class when it comes to defending things they have said in the past leaves me speechless. I'm surprised Boris Johnson didn't cite his right to 'creative licence', which he uses so often to defend his lengthy list of contentious and bigoted remarks.

According to several independent fact-checking services, the figure of £350 million was approximately what the UK gave to the EU before the rebate was deducted. David Norgrove was repeatedly proven to be correct, but Boris stuck to the £350 million figure until 11 September 2019, when he suddenly altered his position. He posted on Twitter that 'Corbyn's #SurrenderBill would mean more pointless Brexit delay at the extra cost of £250m a week', but even this figure doesn't take into account the £90 million that the EU spent in the UK each week. I'm not sure Boris knows when he's telling the truth – he's part of a ruling class that sees itself as untouchable and loses track of its own catalogue of lies.

While we're talking about ministers wilfully disseminating disinformation to deceive the public, stand up Theresa May and Amber Rudd! Their guilt in the Windrush scandal, which broke in 2018, is entirely unforgivable, though the injustice really began in 2012 and is steeped in centuries of xenophobia and racism. The then home secretary Theresa May introduced an administrative measure that even Darth Vader would have been reluctant to implement: the 'hostile environment' policy. The plan was to make it as hard as possible for people without indefinite leave to remain to stay in the UK. The application procedure became even more complicated and fees for processing documents rose dramatically.

The policies introduced by Theresa May effectively transformed ordinary citizens, from doctors to charity workers, into immigration enforcement officers. This was a similar tactic to the Prevent duty, which obliges university lecturers and health professionals to act as surveillance officers on behalf of the state. May's plan made identification checks a legal requirement and refused universal services to people who could not prove that they had the right to reside in the UK. That was followed up by 'Operation Vaken' in the summer of 2013: billboard vans bearing the bold message 'Go Home or Face Arrest' appeared around neighbourhoods with a high number of ethnic minorities. Anyway, who has the right to call Britain home? When children born here to first-generation immigrants are not safe from having their citizenship revoked, who is?

Theresa May's hostile environment policy was just the latest in the series of regular ways in which those in power have neglected the everyday lives of migrants and people of colour. The legal status of the members of the 'Windrush generation' – the nearly half a million people who moved to Britain from the Caribbean between 1948 and 1970, with the first of them arriving on HMT *Empire Windrush* – was flipped overnight. They suddenly required evidence to continue working, collect pensions or receive NHS treatment, despite most of them having arrived through their parents' passports and having had no reason to apply for their own travel documents since then.

The scandal hit the newspapers in November 2017, when the *Guardian* published the stories of several members of the Windrush generation who had been aggressively threatened with deportation, sacked for not having valid documentation or denied medical treatment. The fact that these heart-breaking stories did not lead to universal outrage is a complete travesty. It was a gross error that would have brought down the government in a genuinely fair and equal society — had they not resigned out of embarrassment. Though minorities begged for remedial justice, the media rapidly shifted its focus to new talking points and the government escaped scot-free.

However, one week in April 2018 changed everything. Amid mounting pressure, Home Secretary Amber Rudd issued a cold and empty statement apologising for the treatment of the Windrush generation, telling the House of Commons that it was 'appalling' and 'wrong' that some of them faced deportation. In a direct rebuttal, the Labour MP David Lammy delivered a blistering speech that echoed around the walls of parliament and etched itself in the minds of law-makers and viewers alike, which concluded:

> This is a day of national shame, and it has come about because of a hostile environment policy that was begun under her prime minister. Let us call it like it is. If you lie down with dogs you get fleas, and that is what has happened with this far-right rhetoric in this country. Can she apologise properly? Can she explain how quickly this team will act to ensure that the thousands of British men and women denied their rights in this country under her watch in the Home Office are satisfied?

The next day, at a meeting with 12 Caribbean leaders in Downing Street, Theresa May apologised for the hurt caused to victims. But later that evening it emerged that during her own tenure as home secretary in October 2010, thousands of landing slips documenting the entry of Caribbean immigrants into the UK during the 1950s and 1960s had been destroyed. For some people, these would have been the only proof of when and where they had arrived.

The Home Office argued that the destruction of these landing cards had no impact on the rights of people to stay in the UK, but this was undermined when two whistleblowers revealed that staff routinely used landing card information as part of their decision-making process. Theresa May's attempt to cover up the scandal had ended in resounding failure.

The Tory government was compelled to acknowledge that their policy had led to the wrongful detention, deportation and denial of legal rights of Windrush migrants. Many of them had become prisoners in their own country, unemployed and without access to essential healthcare and hard-earned pensions. But Home Secretary Amber Rudd didn't resign until 29 April, after a leaked memorandum left her denial that there were migrant deportation targets in tatters. The greatest political disruptors are driven by their belief in humanity and their desire for justice, while the most conniving of career politicians will compromise any principles before they cede their grip on power.

Even when they have been repeatedly offered opportunities to put right historical injustices, the Tories have time and again displayed a preference to defer any restorative action. An example of such is their woeful inability to grant an inquiry into the violence perpetrated by South Yorkshire Police on striking miners at the Orgreave coking plant on 18 June 1984. That terrible day was three months into the nationwide industrial action to resist the pit closures being enforced by Thatcher's government. Chilling images of mounted, armoured policemen charging into crowds, while shielded officers beat miners lying prone on the ground, have been etched into public consciousness, with the 'Battle of Orgreave' seared into local folklore. It wasn't just a national disgrace – it was state-led violent repression of the working class.

But typically of the abuses of power that implicate those at the top, no single official was considered to be at fault. No policemen were charged for their violent actions, and no senior officers were punished for their reprehensible instructions. In contrast, 71 pickets were accused of rioting, with 24 charged with violent disorder. Fifteen eventually stood trial, but the cases collapsed after evidence emerged of witness intimidation, statements altered by senior officers and testimonies of junior officers that had been dictated by their corrupt superiors.

Here enters the infamous Peter Wright, who was Chief Constable of South Yorkshire Police at the time. He was not held to account then, and nor has he been in the decades since. In 1991, South Yorkshire Police paid £425,000 in damages to 39 miners who sued for wrongful arrest, assault, unlawful detention and malicious prosecution, but the force still did not admit liability. The families of the victims whose lives were irretrievably ruined have never been granted justice or closure. A report from the Independent Police Complaints Commission in 2015 found evidence of perjury and perversion of the course of justice, but they refused to launch a formal investigation because it was supposedly 'not in the public interest' and 'too much time had elapsed' since the incident. They can rest assured that the children of Orgreave will disrupt for as long as necessary and until justice is delivered.

In September 2016, Amber Rudd met with members of the Orgreave Truth and Justice Campaign. Nevertheless, on 31 October 2016, she ruled out an inquiry on the basis that 'ultimately there were no deaths or wrongful convictions'. Politicians are experts at offering symbolic gestures without making tangible commitments – for them, it's about convenience and those they seek to protect rather than redress for the oppressed.

THE ART OF DISRUPTION

Justice for Orgreave naturally became the focus of one of my monthly campaigns. On 1 August 2018, which was Yorkshire Day, having first sought the blessing of long-term campaigners, I sent this letter to Sajid Javid,[5] or 'The Saj', as he apparently calls himself.

> Ey up Saj,
>
> S'upiwiya?
>
> Our Orgreave miners and their families have been waiting too long. It's time they were given the justice they are owed for all their suffering, all their pain and all their hurt!
>
> 95 miners, 34 years and still no justice!
>
> Now, I know your government is famous for ruining lives, but if you have a heart, you'll do the right thing for once and give the miners and their families a proper, decent and fair inquiry.
>
> Gi'oer with your rubbish,
>
> Lividly,
>
> Magid

---

[5] Sajid Javid was appointed home secretary on 30 April 2018 after Amber Rudd resigned in the wake of the Windrush scandal.

Just like when I challenged him to a charity wrestling match during my appearance on *The Russell Howard Hour*, Mr Javid did not reply.

The focus of one of my monthly campaigns, in January 2019, was one of our country's most significant achievements, and what in my eyes is one of the pinnacles of human progress: the NHS. My post signified the what is visible to many – that our country is sleepwalking into a future bereft of our NHS and the universal humanity it fosters. For the past ten years, the Tories have ravaged our vital public health and social care services, through chronic underfunding and privatisation by stealth – as with any public service, when it comes to the NHS they just can't be trusted. However, unlike with many other things, the effects of their rapacious negligence towards our healthcare system will be felt by our country's majority and not just the most vulnerable.

Boris Johnson promised to add 50,000 new nurses to the workforce in the Conservative manifesto that was published before the general election in December 2019. However, further scrutiny of this claim revealed that the figure included 18,500 who were already working in the NHS and would be encouraged to remain in the profession rather than leave it.

This was malicious misinformation at its peak, with Johnson popularising an arbitrary figure to control the political discourse. Tory manifestos have historically been a collection of empty pledges in an order to win or maintain their grip on power. They have no inherent belief in the values that govern the NHS and no underlying vision for an equal society. There is no political will in them to tackle or even recognise the urgency of the crises before us. Their use of this nurse number tactic or Health Secretary Matt Hancock's deceit around the idea of building 40 new hospitals in the next decade came as no surprise; in the 2015 Conservative manifesto, 5,000 more GPs were promised by 2020, but as of December 2019, there are in fact 1,608 *fewer* full-time GPs. It's up to ordinary people to take the Tories to task for their broken pledges and disrupt the complacency that enables them to not bother following through on their manifesto commitments.

For me, the greatest injustice perpetrated by the Tories is their total inaction in the face of the impending and irreversible climate catastrophe. This is fundamental to why you should keep your lips 100 per cent Tory-free. In June 2019, in one of her final acts as prime minister, Theresa May committed the UK to reduce carbon emissions to 'net-zero' by 2050 – the first member of G7 to do so. However, the pledge comprised few specific details and was, truth be told, an opportunity to garner acclaim while offering no challenge to the fossil-fuel-centred, disaster capitalist economic order. I've learned that with the Tories, it's worth scrutinising anything that may be spun into favourable headlines by an obliging press. Her use of 'net-zero' hinted that the UK would use international carbon credits to pay other countries to cut their carbon emissions but have little ambition to reduce their own. Early in 2020, current prime minister Boris Johnson called on other countries to announce credible targets to reach net zero as quickly as possible. But the fact is he was (and is) still doing nothing to set out firm plans or systematic new measures on how we'll reach the net-zero carbon emissions by 2050 target set out by his predecessor.

Most importantly, making such a commitment for 30 years' time is hardly enough to satisfy the warnings of the October 2018 report by the UN's Intergovernmental Panel on Climate Change. With the report declaring that there were just 12 short years for the world to prevent unprecedentedly deadly levels of warming, Theresa May's ineptitude and the Conservative Party's attitude towards the climate question is brainless. By 2050, the fate for humanity today and for future generations will already be sealed.

This is why groups like Extinction Rebellion and Fridays for Future and leaders like Greta Thunberg are so important, no matter how they are vilified by this government and other bigoted and backward political commentators. This new generation of fearless young activists are fighting to save our planet, fully aware the choice is between action and extinction, and the adults in the room have failed to grasp the urgency of the situation. But the pressure they are exerting and their sheer weight of numbers is forcing politicians to take notice – even the Tories.

* * *

Politicians love to bang on about democracy and how we must protect it at all costs. We saw a lot of this during the Brexit fiasco, like when Boris Johnson told the MPs holding him to account that they were creating a 'people vs parliament' situation, as if he was a champion of popular sovereignty. This was all while he was doing everything he could to protect our outdated model of democracy.

We are living in turbulent times. Across the world, the political institutions of countries that consider themselves democratic are under threat. From Hungary to the US and Honduras to India, democracy is under constant attack from all quarters – whether a biased or negligent media, unchallenged far-right figures, sinister foreign powers or, in the case of the United Kingdom, the Prime Minister himself.

Now, more than ever, democrats of all colours must unite to fight the repressive forces that are threatening to destroy our hard-won freedoms: the notion that a country's future should be decided by its own people and that power should be exercised in the interests of all rather than concentrated in the hands of a select few. In our defence of democracy, we shouldn't just fight to preserve the status quo. It's not about democracy as it is, but as it can and should be.

There are three areas I would focus on to change our democracy for the better. Firstly, we need to empower the youth. Lowering the voting age to 16 is fundamental to ensuring a society with democracy at its core. Giving young people the right to vote will mean they are more likely to take an interest in politics, develop the habit of voting and pay more attention to everything happening around them. Furthermore, with more young people as active participants in our democracy, policymakers will be compelled to take their concerns seriously. Our school curriculum should also emphasise democracy as the cornerstone of our freedoms, highlighting the struggle to achieve it, the critical need to preserve it and the importance of participation in it. Education is the foundation of democracy and should impart an understanding of the process.

The second thing I would institute is a more representative democracy. If we are to make our elections more representative, we have to move away from the first-past-the-post voting system to a form of proportional representation. This change is long overdue, and our unrepresentative system goes a long way towards explaining our current constitutional turmoil. Parliament must reflect the will of the voters; a system that allows every single vote to count, regardless of where you live or who you vote for, will enrich and strengthen our democracy. There are other ways in which the UK Parliament could better reflect the electorate. There is currently a disproportionately low number of representatives from ethnic minority and working-class backgrounds, and that must change; true representation means people of all backgrounds seeing themselves among their elected officials.

The third initiative I would start is to bring about what I call 'a democratic way of life'. Democracy is more than just a form of government – it should place all our communities at the centre of decision-making and aim to achieve wider, communal goals. It should extend to other areas of our lives, like the workplace and even the prison system. Polling day should be a national holiday – there are few better ways of making voting more accessible and highlighting the importance of democracy. Extending democracy into people's lives means giving them the power to make policy rather than being on the receiving end of other people's decisions. The introduction of citizens' assemblies and participatory budgeting exercises would bring democracy to life for everyone. But to truly instil a democratic way of life, we must acknowledge that our decisions have an impact on all living things and on the planet itself. We must govern with that at the forefront of our minds.

Like countless other people, I grew up with the impression that you had to be educated at the most prestigious institutions, be a fantastic public speaker and possess huge wealth to get anywhere in politics, but the truth is that the secret is in the sincerity. It's not actually about becoming a politician – it's about activism as a route to meaningful disruption and change. Though it is often hijacked during selfish attempts to obtain and wield power, politics is part of the journey rather than the end goal. There will always be something you want to change or something new you wish to introduce; we all have our causes, even if we haven't found them yet. Find your cause – and if you're unsure what it is, open yourself up to new experiences so it can find you. And then learn as you go and be ready for the struggle.

But most radically of all, whatever you do, be sure never to kiss a Tory!

IX
TELL YA MA YOU LOVE HER

'No song or poem will bear my mother's name. Yet so many of the stories that I write, that we all write, are my mother's stories.'

Alice Walker

It's important to tell the people you love that you love them. I don't usually call my mum as often as she would like, but she's never far from my thoughts. Due to underlying health conditions she has been sheltering at home throughout the pandemic and so I've been calling her practically every day asking if she needs anything or has any errands she'd like me to run. She always has a lot and as a result we have become much closer. When I set up my first business after university, I named the company Amina – her name. She lives with my sister Hanan, and they're my greatest cheerleaders, but sometimes this enthusiasm has been slightly misguided. When I became lord mayor, my mother was so excited that you'd forgive her for thinking that I had some sort of magic wand where with just a wave of the wand, I could make anything happen in Sheffield. Any issues her friends had, "oh Magid will be able to sort that out now he's lord mayor of Sheffield. I'll never forget when she asked me 'now that you're lord mayor, can you raise the minimum wage in Sheffield?'. If only mum. If only. Still, I can't fault their love, support and enthusiasm.

For some reason (she has certainly never asked for it), I've always dreamt of buying my mum a house to thank her for everything she's done for me. I want to give her a place she can call her own, with a nice garden so she can continue her passion for growing fruit that has no earthly business in a Sheffield flowerbed. If I ever do manage to, I think she'd probably say to me, joking yet seriously, 'If you want to acknowledge my sacrifices, get married and have some children. I don't need a house!' She ideally wants me to marry a Somali girl, and she has lots of them in mind. She'll often say things like, 'Ooh, so-and-so's daughter is beautiful and not married, do you want me to introduce you to her? She's a nice girl.' Either that or she'll try and send me on a fake errand to meet some friends of hers who will just so happen to have a female relative of about the same age as me. Thankfully, at the moment she's stopped this talk of marriage for now, though maybe it will start happening again when I get closer to 35 . . .

I know she loves me and is proud of me, even if she'd secretly rather I was a doctor, lawyer or engineer, but that's only because she wants the best for me – and to her that means stability. The life I've chosen is unpredictable, but that's part of the reason I love it. You see for her, true happiness has never been anything material. It's seeing her children happy and do well in this life, and as Muslims, life in the hereafter. And I don't think I'll truly understand that kind of love and happiness until I'm hopefully blessed to have children of my own one day. I could never thank my mum enough for her sacrifices that give me the freedom to make that choice, but in my inauguration speech when I became lord mayor, I took the opportunity to say the many things I felt she deserved to hear:

> When you look at me, I don't want you to see this chain or this robe or this magnificent chamber we are currently in: I want you to see, or at least try and imagine, all the people that played a pivotal role in this story that is unfolding today.
>
> But most important of all, when you look at me I want you to see that woman there. 'Hooyo [mother], please stand up.' You have probably walked past her in the street many times and never noticed her. The racists and Islamophobes probably have the worst things to say about her, but they don't even know her. But because of my mother's countless sacrifices, from leaving Somalia with

only courage, hope, determination and children in her hands, to making sure that me and my sister never neglected our education, from dealing with all her own personal struggles and challenges, as well as having to put up with some of the shit I put her through as a teenager, she still never lost faith in me, and I am standing here because of her.

Hooyo macaan, my dearest mother. You made this possible. I know you've been through a lot, and I know I've personally put you through a lot. May God protect you, may God make it so that others see you with the love that I see you, and may I use the love you have given me to give love to others. This is all about you, all this – this is for you. And I hate to break it to you, hooyo, but I don't think I'll be getting married anytime soon, so this is as big as it gets, Mum. Lap it up.

In that speech, I also spoke about friends of mine who have become more like family in Sheffield. People like Abdi, who I met when we were both students' union presidents – me at Hull and him at Sheffield. He is the exception to the unwritten rule 'don't hire your friends' and has been my right-hand man in Brussels for the past year. Abdi's main interests are hot air ballooning, artificial intelligence and using politics to bring about positive change. He remembers everything and often dispenses random yet weirdly compelling facts without being asked, which means he gets wound up a bit in the office. Like me, the term 'office hours' is alien to him. We're both driven by the cause and often burn the midnight oil. Not only is he one of the smartest people I know, he's also been a true friend in every sense of the word. He challenges me to go further, isn't afraid to get his hands dirty and most importantly, he always has my back! He's someone I completely trust. We are bonded by our shared love for fighting fascists, eating ribs and working towards creating a more compassionate world.

We must always tell our friends that we love them, too. I also mentioned my friend Ahmed, who also came to Sheffield from Somalia, but a bit later than we did. He probably understands me more than anyone else, because we share the experience of finding ourselves in a new country, knowing no one and not speaking the language. Sometimes I feel too foreign to be either British or Somali, and he gets that. As kids we both made friends in Sheffield in spite of that, when we found that children don't care what language you can speak, as long as you can have a laugh and kick a football. Over time, we learned how to navigate our way through society with multiple identities.

Ahmed is like a brother to me and we sometimes still talk to each other in Somali, which usually involves insulting each other and telling various in-jokes that no one else understands – the kind of things that show we care, in a funny way. He's an engineer and married with a child – come to think of it, he's a lot of things my mum wants me to be!

I love Sheffield – some of the best folk live here and many of them have treated me like their son, grand-son or brother from the first time we met. Being born 6,500 miles away, I could never have known that this city would come to mean so much to me. Though I am not originally from here, it has made me who I am. From the hills to the rivers, from the trees to the tramlines, from the Blades to the Owls, in the rain, the snow and the sunshine, Sheffield will always be my home.

Let's be honest – from the outside, mine is an unlikely story. I'm a black, Muslim refugee who became the youngest lord mayor in the history of Sheffield. But those of us who live here know that mine is just one of thousands of unlikely stories made possible by the kindness of neighbours, teachers, friends and strangers. Strangers matter more in Sheffield than in most cities, and anyone who lives here has probably had their heart warmed by a gentle conversation at the bus stop about the weather, sport or about how everything is Maggie Thatcher's fault (which it definitely is).

Strangers matter in Sheffield, but sooner or later it becomes clear that they don't really exist – we all know someone who knows someone who knows the person we think is a stranger. It was this idea that helped me discover a burning passion to fight injustice. A lot of the bad things in the world might look like they are happening far away and to strangers, but in Sheffield we are never that far from the world's stage, and there are people here who are connected to people all over the world. That's why I think it is no accident that Sheffield became the first City of Sanctuary in the UK. Connection, welcome and respect are all built into the place – they are in our DNA.

It is easy to think of Sheffield through the eyes of the outside world – as a post-industrial, mid-sized city, somewhere up North, made notable by *The Full Monty*, Pulp, Prince Naseem, the Arctic Monkeys and Sean Bean. Though I do like our local celebs, I see our city completely differently. Sheffield has been at the heart of British life for hundreds of years. Many of the miners who fought Thatcher's government lived here and Robin Hood, or 'Robin of Loxley', was one of us too. But beyond that, chartists, suffragettes and radicals of all types emerged from our city and changed the country for ever.

The truth is that this dedication to helping each other, the world and the environment is just as alive today as ever before, despite what some of our leaders might wish. During my time in office, I met pupils, students, teachers, artists, intellectuals, social workers and carers from every corner of the city and the world. These people inspired me every day, showing me the meaning of kindness, care and dedication to something bigger than themselves. They reminded me what I was here to honour, protect and remember. Even though the struggle for tolerance and compassion is far from over, it is this city's character that gives me hope.

I'm so grateful that we made that 6,500-mile journey to this place, and it would not have happened were it not for the sacrifice, courage and determination of my mother. She is the person whose smiles will always mean the most to me, the person who has taught me that love and hope are vast enough to envelop the world.

Every mother has made sacrifices for you. You might not have any idea about some of those sacrifices yet. But you will one day, so make sure you tell her you love her. And maybe pick up the phone once in a while.

X
YOU'VE GOT THIS!

'When you get these jobs that you have been so brilliantly trained for, just remember that your real job is that if you are free, you need to free somebody else. If you have some power, then your job is to empower somebody else.'

Toni Morrison

My past couple of years as an activist and politician have shown me that there is always hope, even in the most obscure of places. And courage is contagious; don't ever underestimate the impact you can have on others. Every time you take a stand, challenge the status quo or do things differently, not only will your hope take a life of its own but you will also excite and empower those around you. But standing up takes energy, and we all need coping mechanisms to help us see the hope, whether that be yoga, praying or drawing. For me, despite what my dentist or my waistline tells me, that mechanism is cake. Any form of cake or pudding will do, my favourite being hot flapjack and lots of custard! If you can provide such a delicious treat for a friend in need, I can't imagine it would go unappreciated.

Most importantly, you need compassion – it should be at the heart of everything we do. Yes, we are living through difficult times, and we may encounter events and people that infuriate us. But we need to be strong, be understanding, work collaboratively and most importantly of all, show compassion, the ultimate manifestation of strength.

It's all well and good me writing this book as someone who's achieved what I have, but I'm not arrogant enough to think that I did it by myself. And I'd be lying if I said I achieved it through hard work alone, as we all know that hard work alone doesn't get you far enough. If I had an equation, it would be: Hard work + sacrifice + courage + opportunity − shit-throwing = achieving your goals.

My success is as much about other people, including you, the readers of this book, as it is about me. Had it not been for my mother who sacrificed everything for me, the friends who grounded me, the people who voted for me and the countless strangers who have shown me unwavering support, this story would have not been told. And yes, my story is inspiring, I get that. But what does it inspire you to do?

If we want our local people to engage in politics and trust their politicians, they need to start seeing themselves in their representatives. We need unapologetic working-class voices, but also voices from diverse backgrounds, ethnicities and genders. To see an authentic representation of yourself among your political representatives is incredibly empowering.

For transformative change to be possible, politics needs to move away from upper- and middle-class white men in suits who claim to work for ordinary people. We also need to use our platform to highlight injustices and raise awareness around issues that matter. That's our duty as public servants.

You don't have to have a fancy title like 'lord mayor' or 'MEP' to bring about the positive change you want to see – a lot of people who inspire me aren't politicians. Find out what it is you're good at, and don't be afraid to step out of your comfort zone. If you're a writer, try to get something published. If you're funny, try stand-up comedy. If you're angry with the status quo and are good at encouraging people to join a cause you believe in, stand for election. If you love technology, think of ways you could use it to engage people. We have to win the cultural struggle as well as the political struggle, either by being elected or by changing the minds of those who have been.

This year I've witnessed a lot of people, saying that their situation is hopeless, saying things like 'this government isn't listening, we can't win, I'm giving up'. But that is exactly what they want us to believe and do. We can't afford to enter into a state of despair. Despair is not an option for me, for you, for all our loved ones or for the future of our planet. The problems we face didn't just come down from the heavens, they are made by bad human decisions. Mainly by men in suits. Good human decisions can change everything, for the better. As powerful as the elites and corporations are, when we stand up and refuse to be divided not only will they not stop us but there's nothing we can't achieve.

Recent global events have transformed what is politically possible. The Coronavirus has exposed not only the deep inequality within our society but has also proven what many progressives have been arguing for years: we are only as secure as the most vulnerable amongst us. Any argument to the contrary has fallen apart. For years we were told that the government was trying really hard but that it just wasn't possible to house all homeless people. Then the pandemic hit and they housed the homeless. For years we were told that the government couldn't borrow beyond a certain point. Then the pandemic hit and they borrowed record amounts. These are just two examples of many. Every time we were told certain things couldn't be done, we were being lied to. It was complete bollocks. We must use this knowledge and confront governments with it. It was never a question of economics. It has always been a question of political will. We all have to reconsider what's possible and be more ambitious and demand more.

Perspective can change everything. As scary, painful and depressing as 2020 has been so far, it can also be an opportunity that enables us to grow and see the change we desperately need. So rather than accepting this year as a complete shitshow and nothing more, it could prove to be the most important year of all: and it is up to all of us to make this happen.

But transformative change is not spontaneous – it requires people to come together and think of ways to improve the lives of ordinary people, through dignity, humanity and universality. It is our time to step up, answer the urgent questions of our time and build futures that work for both people and our planet. And in these tasks, you'll find me by your side.

You've got this! x

ACKNOWLEDGEMENTS

Before this book, the most I'd ever written was a 2000 word essay explaining how tides occur and their consequences for the marine ecosystem when I was at university. So you can imagine writing a book was not only going to be really challenging but even the prospect of it was ridiculous. As if it wasn't hard enough, writing it while working as an MEP during the height of the Brexit saga was a tall order.

Nonetheless it really wouldn't have been possible without the love, support and encouragement from the beautiful people below who I'll be eternally grateful to.

- Most authors normally have one editor throughout the journey of a book but I've been truly spoiled and have had three. Joel Simmons, thanks for believing in me and the book from the get go and introducing me to the wonderful people at Bonnier. Oliver Holden-Rea, thanks for your commitment, letting me know you also go to gigs by yourself and that it's completely normal. But most of all, thanks for being so frikkin' patient with me. Susannah Otter, you've been nothing short of amazing. Thanks for putting your heart and soul into this and championing the book.

- My incredible publicist, Nikki Mander and marketing manager Jessica Tackie, who had the job of pushing the book out there in the midst of a global pandemic.
- Massive love to Madiya Altaf, Alba Proko and everyone at Bonnier who'd played a role in bringing this book to life.
- Minnie Rahman, for introducing me to the wonderful Grace Pengelly who was the first person to explain to me how the world of publishing worked and helped me start this journey. Thanks a bunch Grace.
- My agent Matthew Turner for just being awesome, always being there and tolerating my unnecessarily long whatsapp voice notes.
- Nathan, for his wisdom, teaching me so much about writing, the Spice Girls and introducing me to baklava sundae.

ACKNOWLEDGEMENTS

- Joshua Forstenzer, there have been many times where I've doubted myself, many times I've hit roadblocks and even times I thought of not going through with the book. But you've always been there and constantly told me that it will all work out. And it has. Thanks for everything bro.
- Mohammed Bux, probably one of the smartest people I've had the pleasure of meeting. You've not only played an integral role in the stories that are in this book but I'm a better person for everything I've learnt from you.
- Kevin Kennedy, Hassun El Zafar and Snoop. You guys have been there throughout this whirlwind journey. Thanks for shaping this book and constantly pushing me to go out of my comfort zone. Also, a special thanks to Kevin for helping design the book cover.
- Alison Teal, for her constant unwavering support, filling in some of my memory blanks when writing and just being a great source of inspiration.
- Areeq Choudry, for always being there to listen to all my struggles about writing and kept believing in me.

- Ahmed Jama, for always keeping it 100 with me and never letting me lose sight of what really matters.
- Dave Crapper from FYI and the Tramlines Festival team for giving me the opportunity to put whatever I wanted on a massive billboard at the festival which became Sheffield's Ten Commandments.
- My wonderful team at the European Parliament, Abdiaziz Suleiman, Aya Delfi, Lara Alagha, Linda Nagy, Rose Birchard and Silvia Carta. You guys have inspired me like you wouldn't imagine. Thanks for always having my back, going above and beyond and reminding me the importance of compassion.
- My dearest mother and sister Hanan, I'll always be grateful for your unconditional love and nonstop support. And Hanan, thanks for showing me the beauty and magic of reading books.
- The European Parliament cleaning staff who would always find me in my office at 5am most mornings of the week writing, thanks for fueling me with hilarious stories, Moroccan tea and encouraging me to keep writing.

ACKNOWLEDGEMENTS

- Veronica Monaghan, Julie Wilson, Adil Zahman and Helen Zefi. I know I was difficult at times but we did have fun. Thanks for all the support, laughs and letting me get away with murder. Love you all.

I'm sure there's some people I've forgotten to mention, but always know that I'm forever grateful.

#Alhamdulillah
#BlackLivesMatter